GreatCentsBooks

For permission requests, please contact:
GreatCents Books
bteich@greatcents.org

Edited by: Blake Teichmeier

Printed in the United States of America.

ISBN: 978-1-971213-09-5

First Edition:

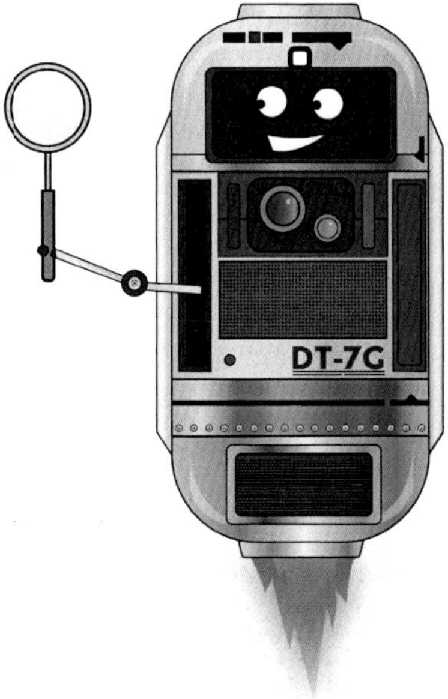

To Mom and Dad, you have been a huge blessing in my life. Thank you for helping me to become the person I am today!

This book is part of the series called **Galactic Growth**. Our goal is to help you think about your **mind & money.**

Who are you dedicating your work on this book to:

Table of Contents

This book belongs to:

Galactic Growth!

Social Emotional Learning
& Personal Finances

Mars

Picking Your Earning Path

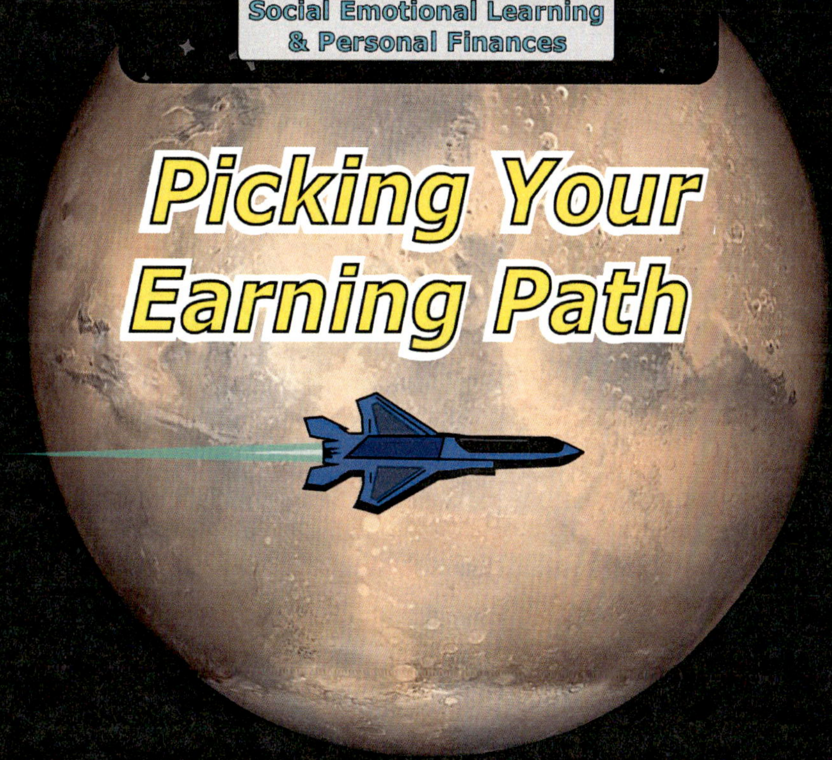

Written and Illustrated by:
Blake Teichmeier

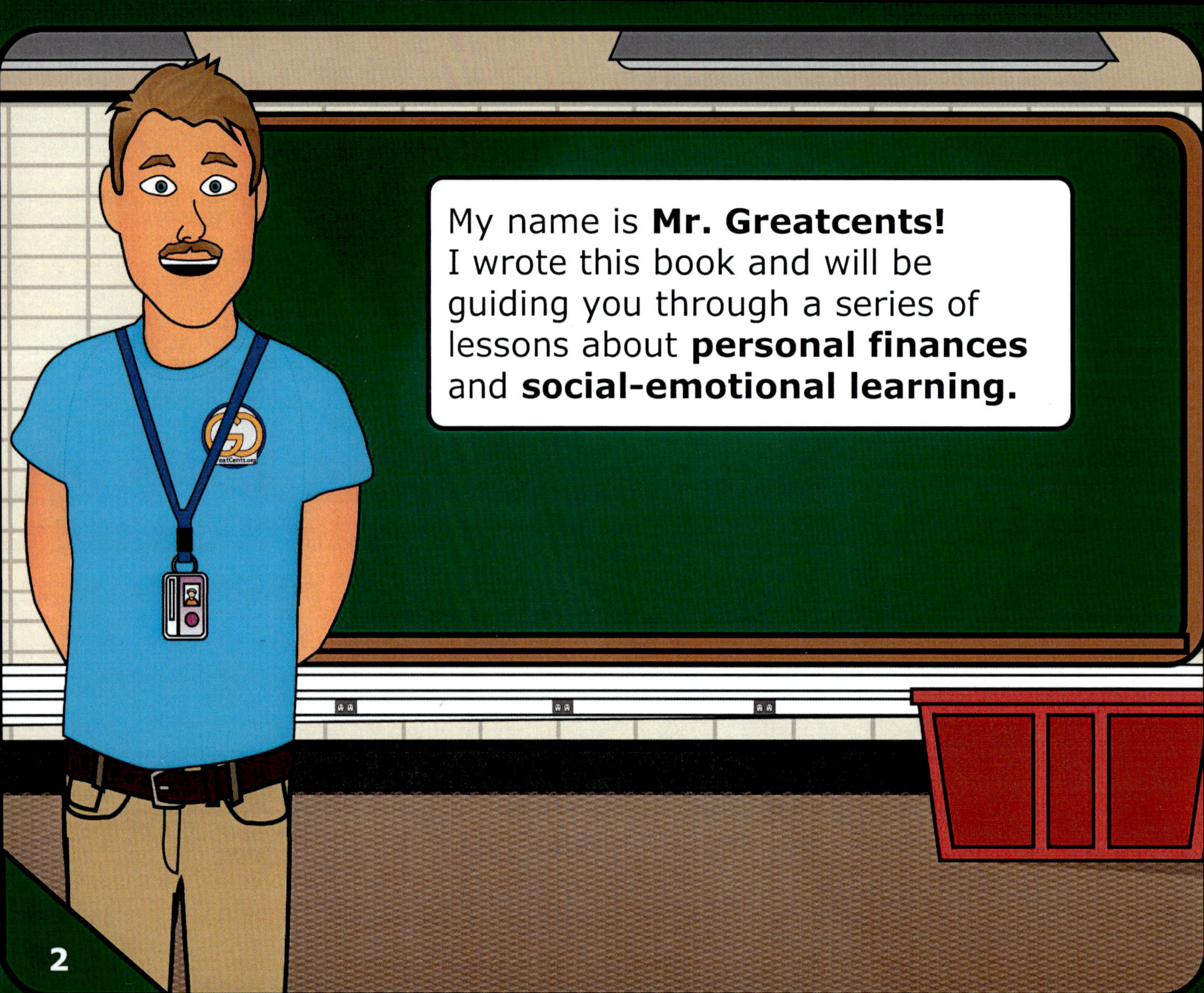
My name is **Mr. Greatcents!**
I wrote this book and will be guiding you through a series of lessons about **personal finances** and **social-emotional learning.**

You are getting older, and with that comes **new responsibilities**. You will need to be more aware of your **mind**, the choices you make, and your **money**, and the way you spend and save your money. Join me as we leave our familiar world behind and venture into a universe of learning!

Everyday you are building skills that will help you in the future! What is a skill you are proud of?

Galactic Growth!

Social Emotional Learning & Personal Finances

Picking Your Earning Path

Our Goal:
Study the connection between **identity**, **personality** and **work**.

Step 1: Describe a person's earning journey.

Step 2: Study identity and identify how you see it guiding your life.

Step 3: Recognize your personality and how it shapes your choices.

Step 4: Connect your multiple intelligences with a future career.

We have some work to do!
We're on our way to Station 4.

Excellent! Beatrix left the Mars rover out for me. She must have been here last. It is so nice when things are where they are supposed to be!

Looks like a big storm is rolling in. I have a few hours before it really hits. Hopefully, I get all my outside tasks done quickly.
U.S.S. CHESTERTON
1988
Beep-Beep!
Yes, we will be safe in the station. It was made to stand up to the worst storms!
8

It's been a while since I've been here. Let's find our task chart and get started!
U.S.S. CHESTERTON
1988
4

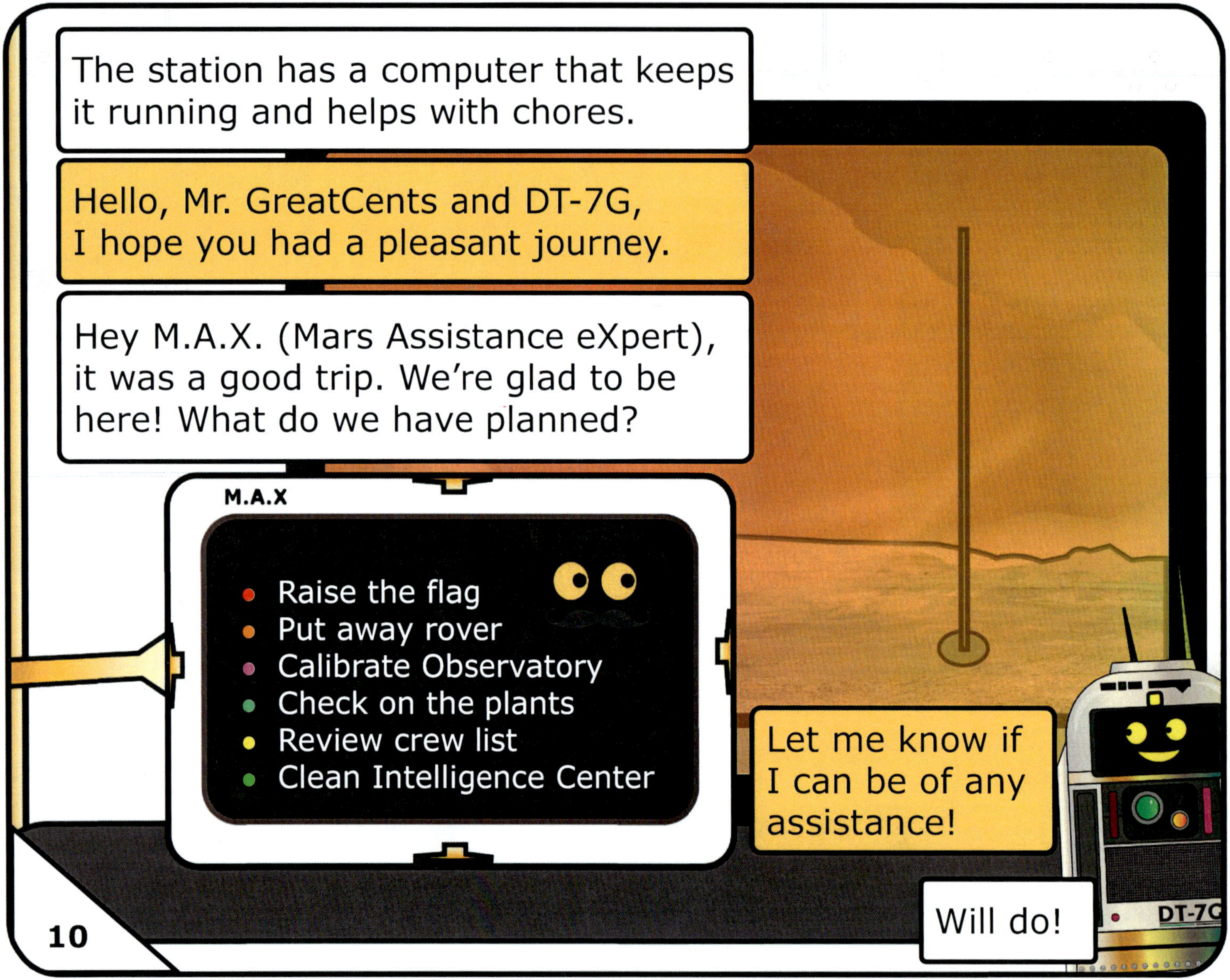

The station has a computer that keeps it running and helps with chores.
Hello, Mr. GreatCents and DT-7G, I hope you had a pleasant journey.
Hey M.A.X. (Mars Assistance eXpert), it was a good trip. We're glad to be here! What do we have planned?
M.A.X
Raise the flag
Put away rover
Calibrate Observatory
Check on the plants
Review crew list
Clean Intelligence Center
Let me know if I can be of any assistance!
Will do!
DT-7G

To get this done, I better prioritize! First, I need to do the outdoor chores. Otherwise, I might run the risk of getting hurt. What are some chores you do at home?

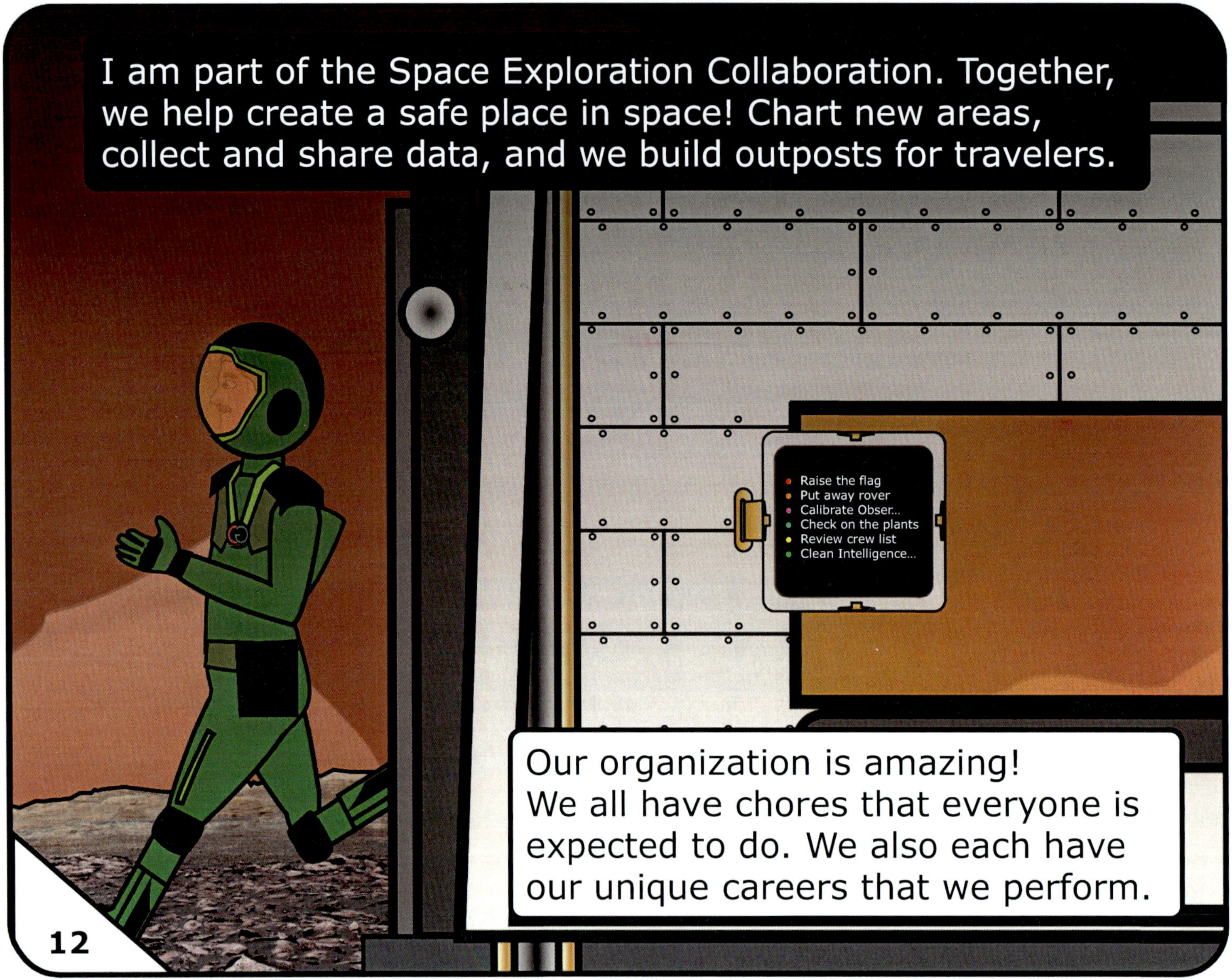
I am part of the Space Exploration Collaboration. Together, we help create a safe place in space! Chart new areas, collect and share data, and we build outposts for travelers.
Raise the flag
Put away rover
Calibrate Obser...
Check on the plants
Review crew list
Clean Intelligence...
Our organization is amazing! We all have chores that everyone is expected to do. We also each have our unique careers that we perform.

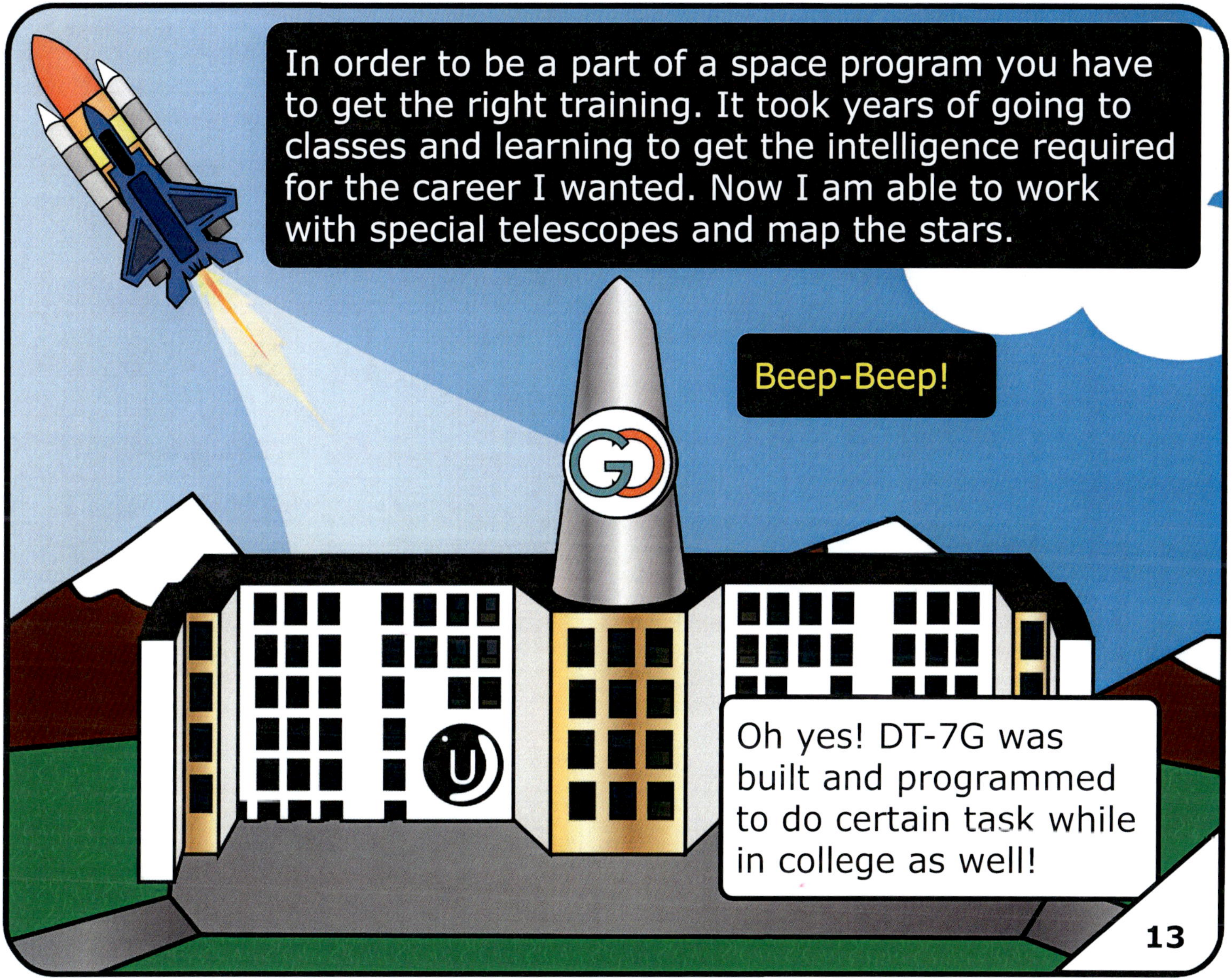
In order to be a part of a space program you have to get the right training. It took years of going to classes and learning to get the intelligence required for the career I wanted. Now I am able to work with special telescopes and map the stars.
Beep-Beep!
Oh yes! DT-7G was built and programmed to do certain task while in college as well!

Let's look at your process when it comes to work as a kid. Let's start with your home. There's always work to be done. This usually falls on the family, and we call them chores!

Chores:
Regular tasks done at home to help out, typically without pay.

Key Word

Here are some examples of chores you can do around your home!
Check any of these you do!

- [ ] Washing dishes
- [ ] Sweeping or vacuuming
- [ ] Taking out the trash
- [ ] Folding laundry
- [ ] Dusting furniture
- [ ] Cleaning the bathroom
- [ ] Feeding pets
- [ ] Helping with dinner
- [ ] Watering plants
- [ ] Making the bed

How do you help at home? Below write down the chore and illustrate it!

Example:
Cleaning up my room.

Picture

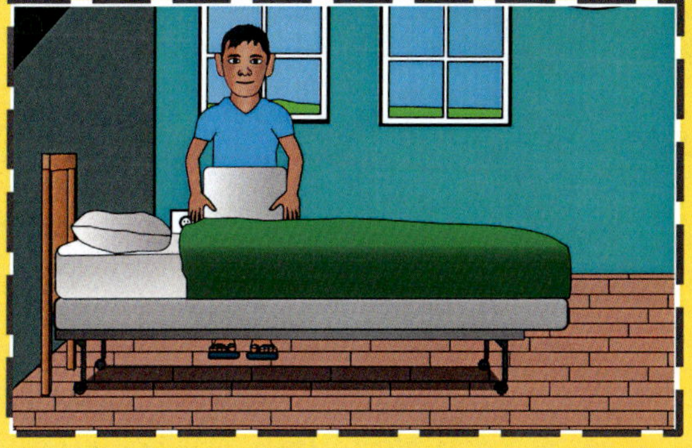

Picture

Picture

Picture

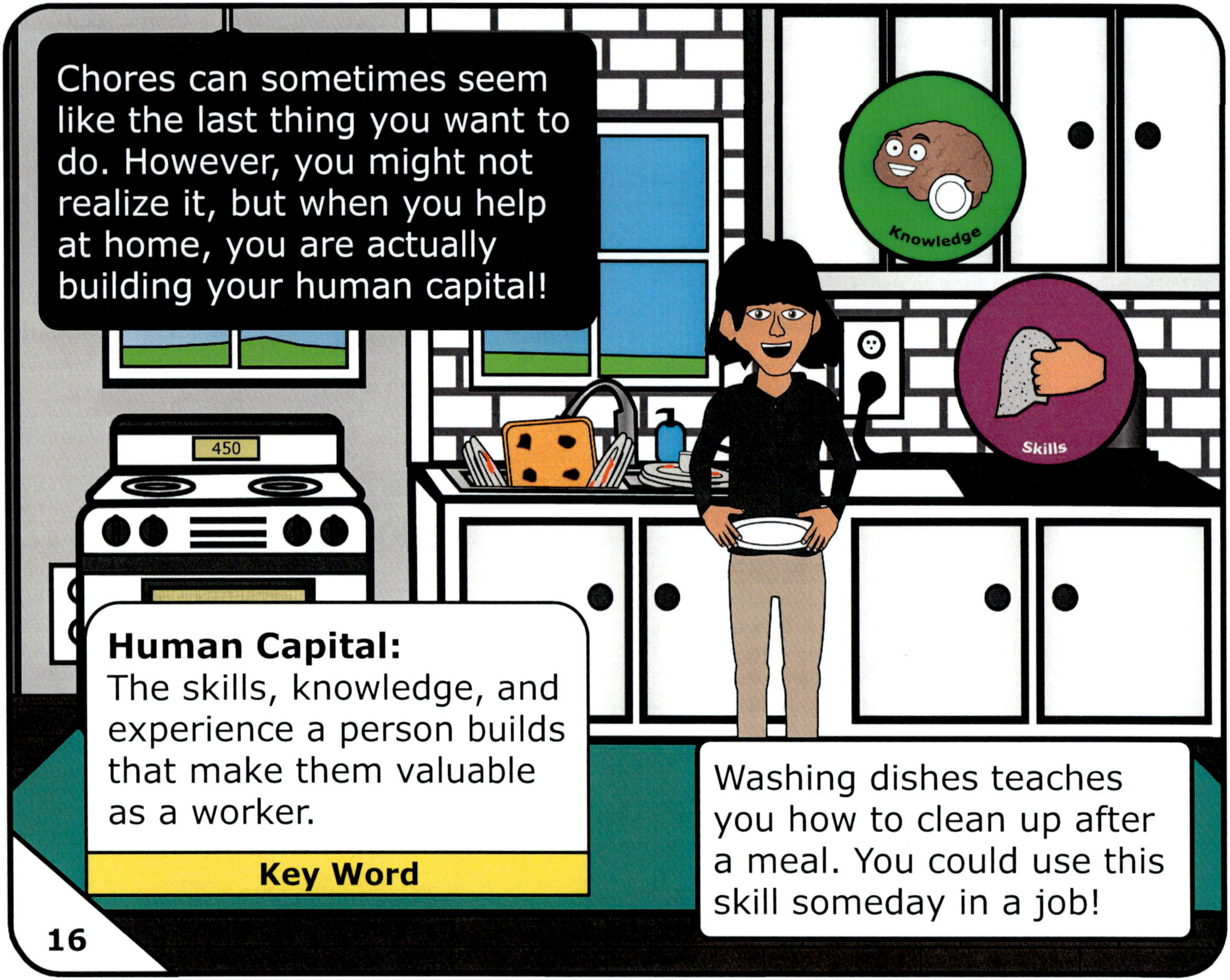
Chores can sometimes seem like the last thing you want to do. However, you might not realize it, but when you help at home, you are actually building your human capital!
Knowledge
Skills
450
Human Capital:
The skills, knowledge, and experience a person builds that make them valuable as a worker.
Key Word
Washing dishes teaches you how to clean up after a meal. You could use this skill someday in a job!

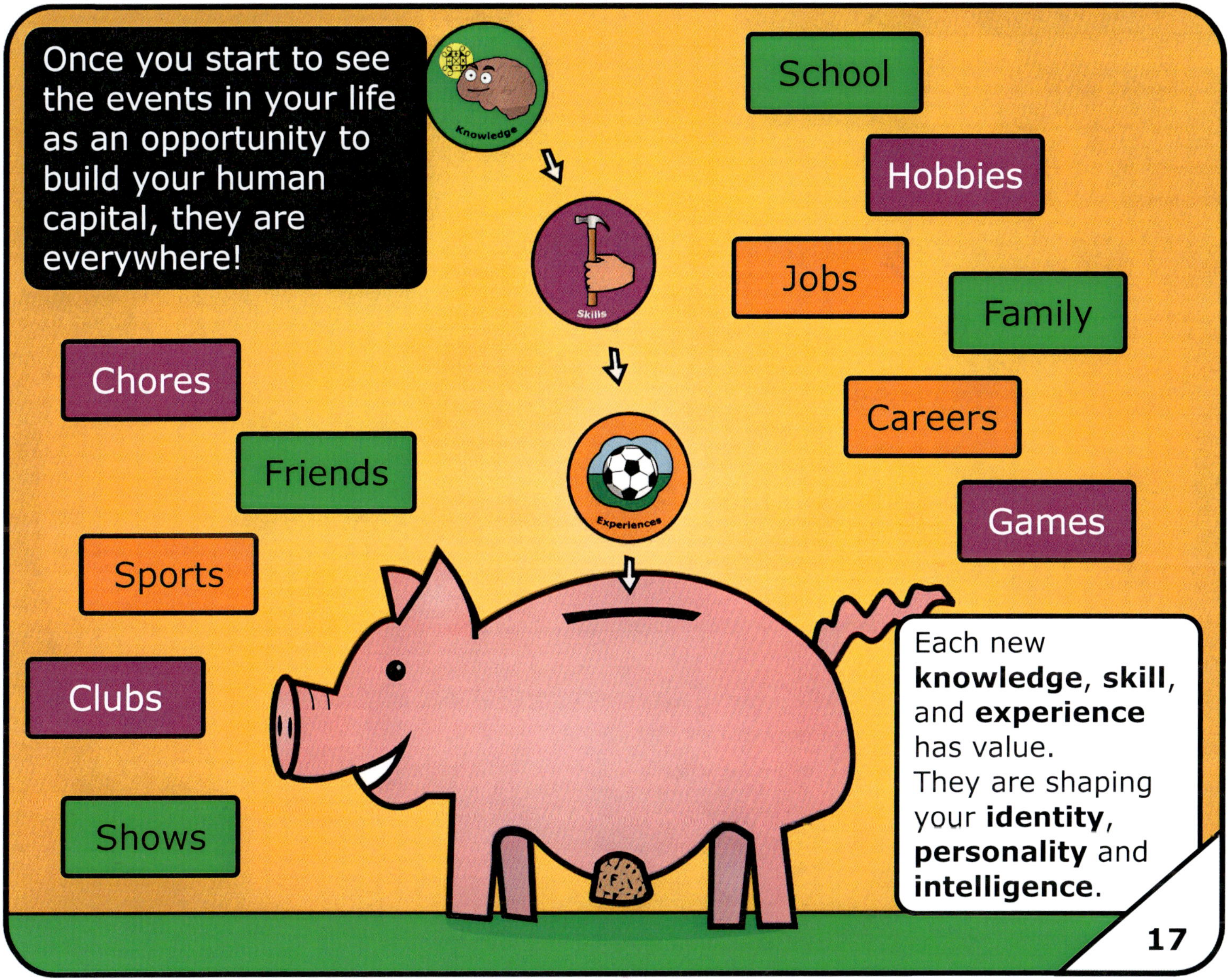
Once you start to see the events in your life as an opportunity to build your human capital, they are everywhere!
Knowledge
Skills
Experiences
School
Hobbies
Jobs
Family
Careers
Games
Chores
Friends
Sports
Clubs
Shows
Each new **knowledge**, **skill**, and **experience** has value. They are shaping your **identity**, **personality** and **intelligence**.

So how can I use my human capital to make money?

We all have **wants** and **needs** and we are willing to pay others to provide for them for us. If you have the right **human capital**, skills, knowledge, and abilities, you can earn money by meeting those needs. We will talk about this more later, but for now it is important to know that the money you earn from working is called **income**.

Income:
The money that a person earns from working, investments, or assistance.

Key Word

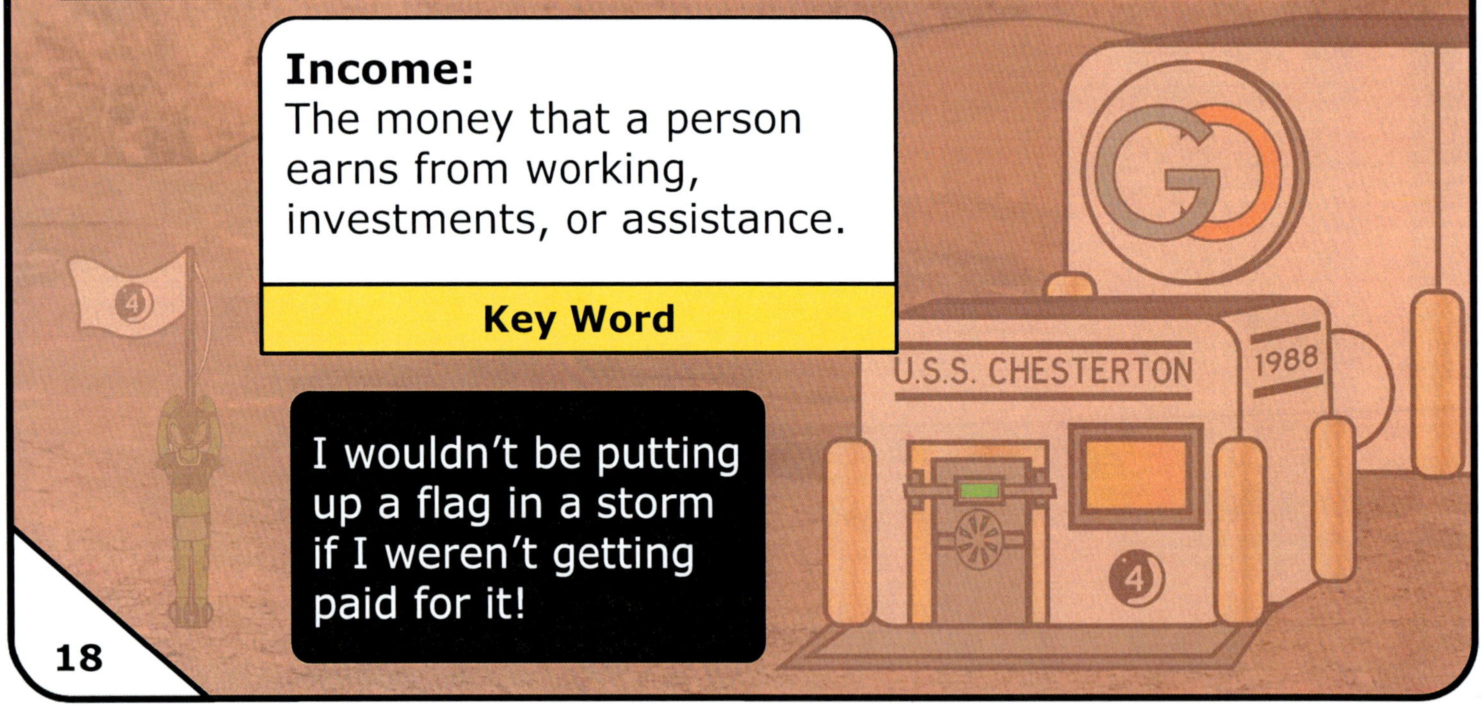

Using your math skills calculate how much these people have earned for their income! (This is called your Gross Pay, we will talk about deductions and Net Pay later!)

Name: Blake
Job: Cashier
Wage: $12
Hours: 10
Income:

Name: Iris
Job: Nurse
Wage: $28
Hours: 20
Income:

Name: Jennifer
Job: Fast Food
Wage: $13
Hours: 12
Income:

Name: Jude
Job: Dog Walker
Wage: $10
Hours: 5
Income:

Name: Pablo
Job: Lawn Mower
Wage: $14
Hours: 8
Income:

Name: Vira
Job: Lifeguard
Wage: $16
Hours: 9
Income:

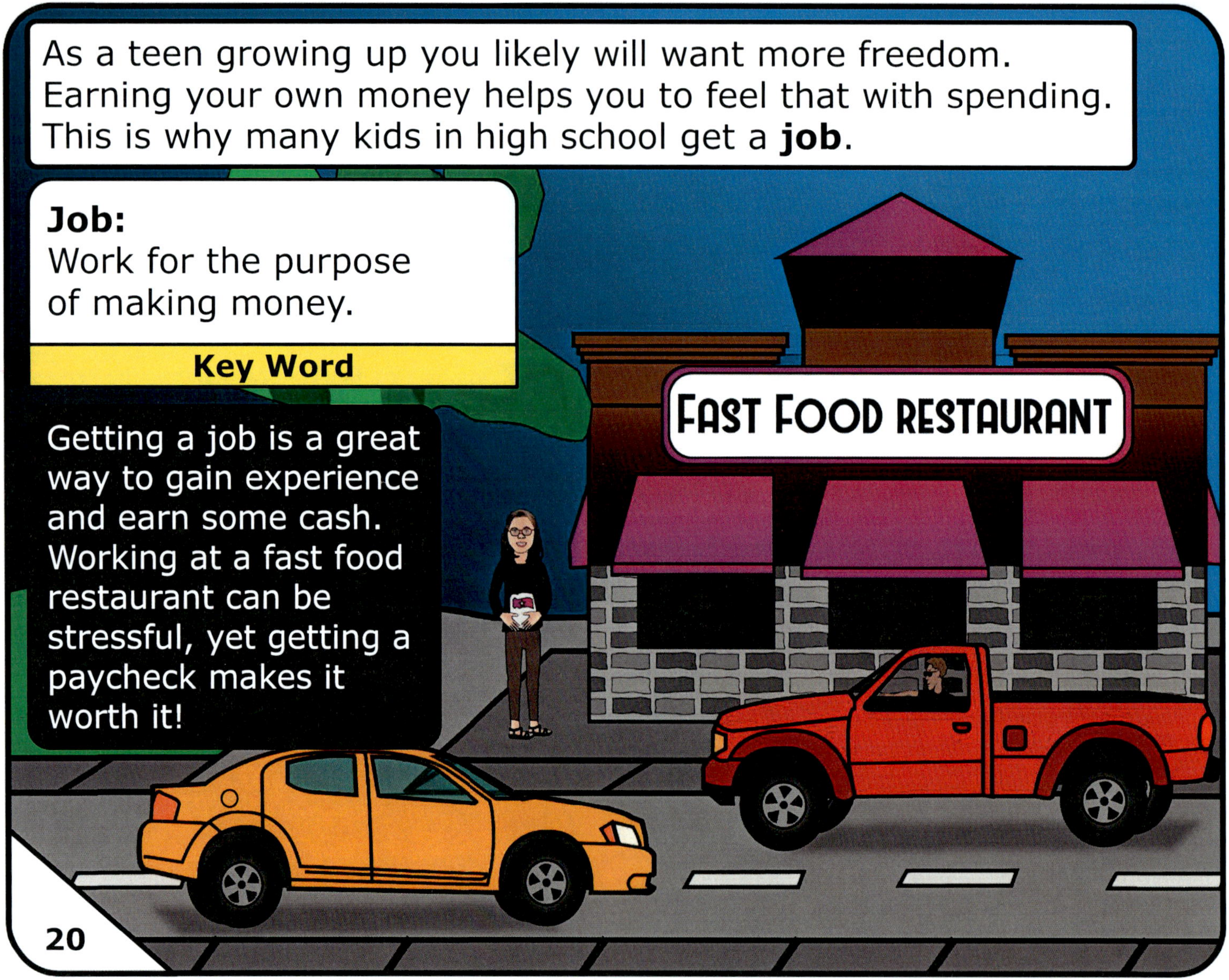
As a teen growing up you likely will want more freedom. Earning your own money helps you to feel that with spending. This is why many kids in high school get a **job**.
Job:
Work for the purpose of making money.
Key Word
Getting a job is a great way to gain experience and earn some cash. Working at a fast food restaurant can be stressful, yet getting a paycheck makes it worth it!
FAST FOOD RESTAURANT

Jobs are a great way to build human capital.
What are 5 jobs that teens can get where you live?
What skills can they build through their work?

Job	Skills learned

Find pictures for some of these jobs:

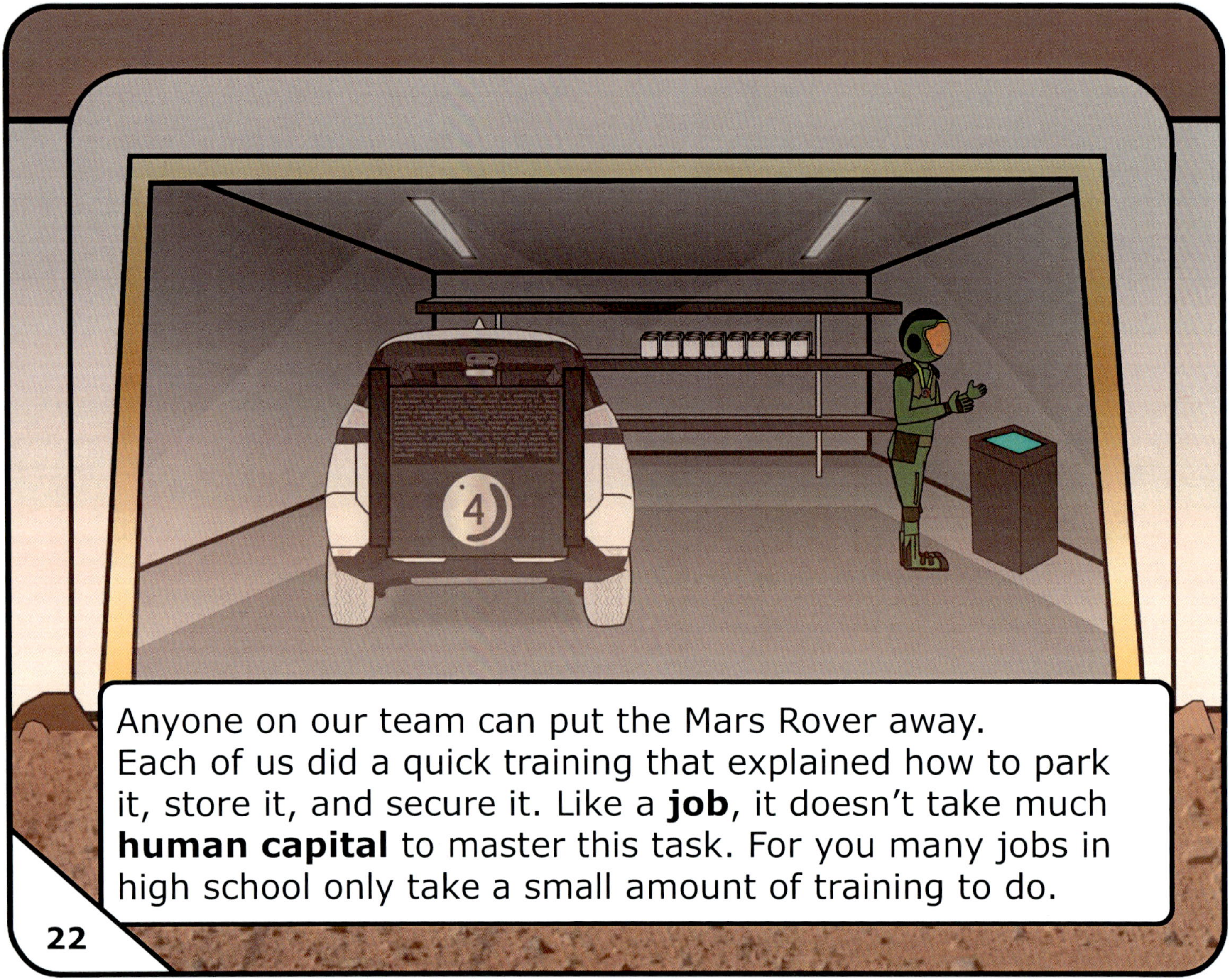
Anyone on our team can put the Mars Rover away. Each of us did a quick training that explained how to park it, store it, and secure it. Like a **job**, it doesn't take much **human capital** to master this task. For you many jobs in high school only take a small amount of training to do.

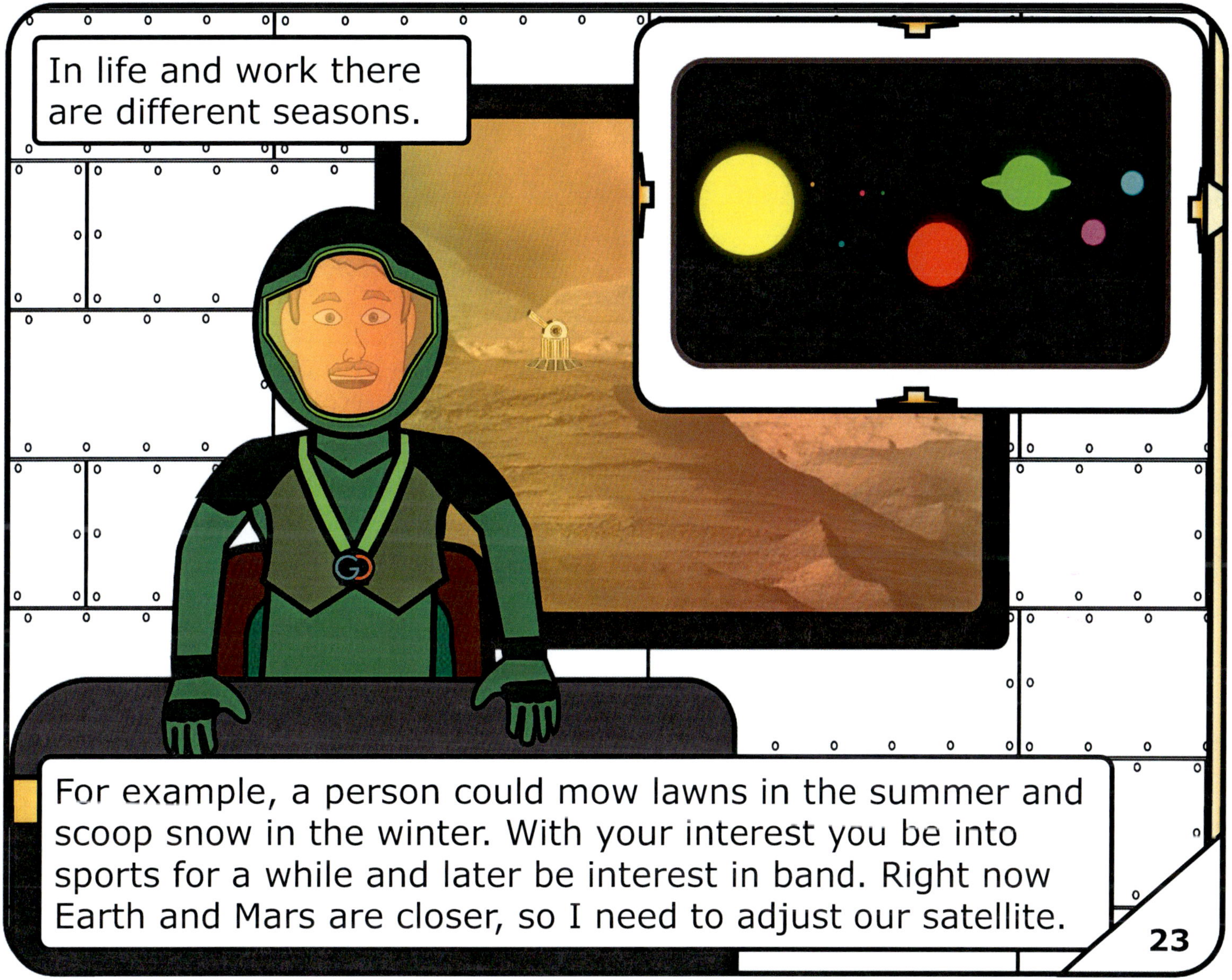
In life and work there are different seasons.
For example, a person could mow lawns in the summer and scoop snow in the winter. With your interest you be into sports for a while and later be interest in band. Right now Earth and Mars are closer, so I need to adjust our satellite.

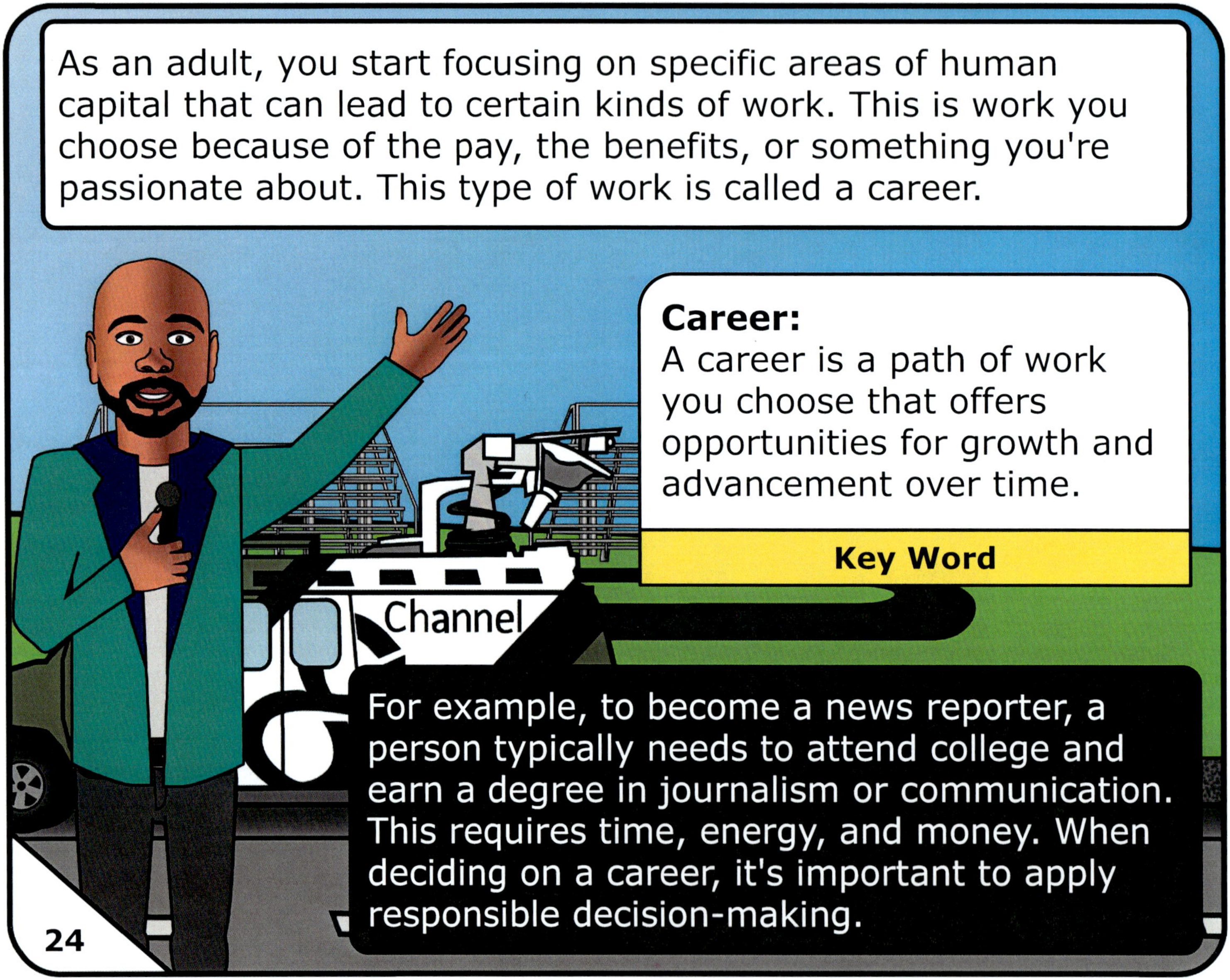
As an adult, you start focusing on specific areas of human capital that can lead to certain kinds of work. This is work you choose because of the pay, the benefits, or something you're passionate about. This type of work is called a career.
Career:
A career is a path of work you choose that offers opportunities for growth and advancement over time.
Key Word
Channel
For example, to become a news reporter, a person typically needs to attend college and earn a degree in journalism or communication. This requires time, energy, and money. When deciding on a career, it's important to apply responsible decision-making.

Careers require higher amounts of human capital. Determine for each career what knowledge and skills they would need:

Nurse

Knowledge:

Skills:

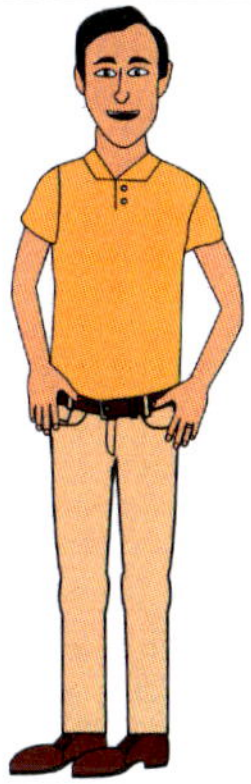

Teacher

Knowledge:

Skills:

Business Owner

Knowledge:

Skills:

Police Officer

Knowledge:

Skills:

Okay, the next task is calibrating the observatory. We will take the elevator to the top.
Observation Deck
I am the only person with the training to do this task. I feel confident because I know what I am doing. Having skills really makes work more enjoyable!

M.A.X
MAX here... The wind outside is currently at 120 miles per hour. It will be unsafe to leave the building again for the next 3 hours. I highly recommend staying inside.
Good to be back inside! Now that my outdoor chores are finished, we have plenty of time to take a break. I would like to share **my earning journey** with you.
This sounds like fun!

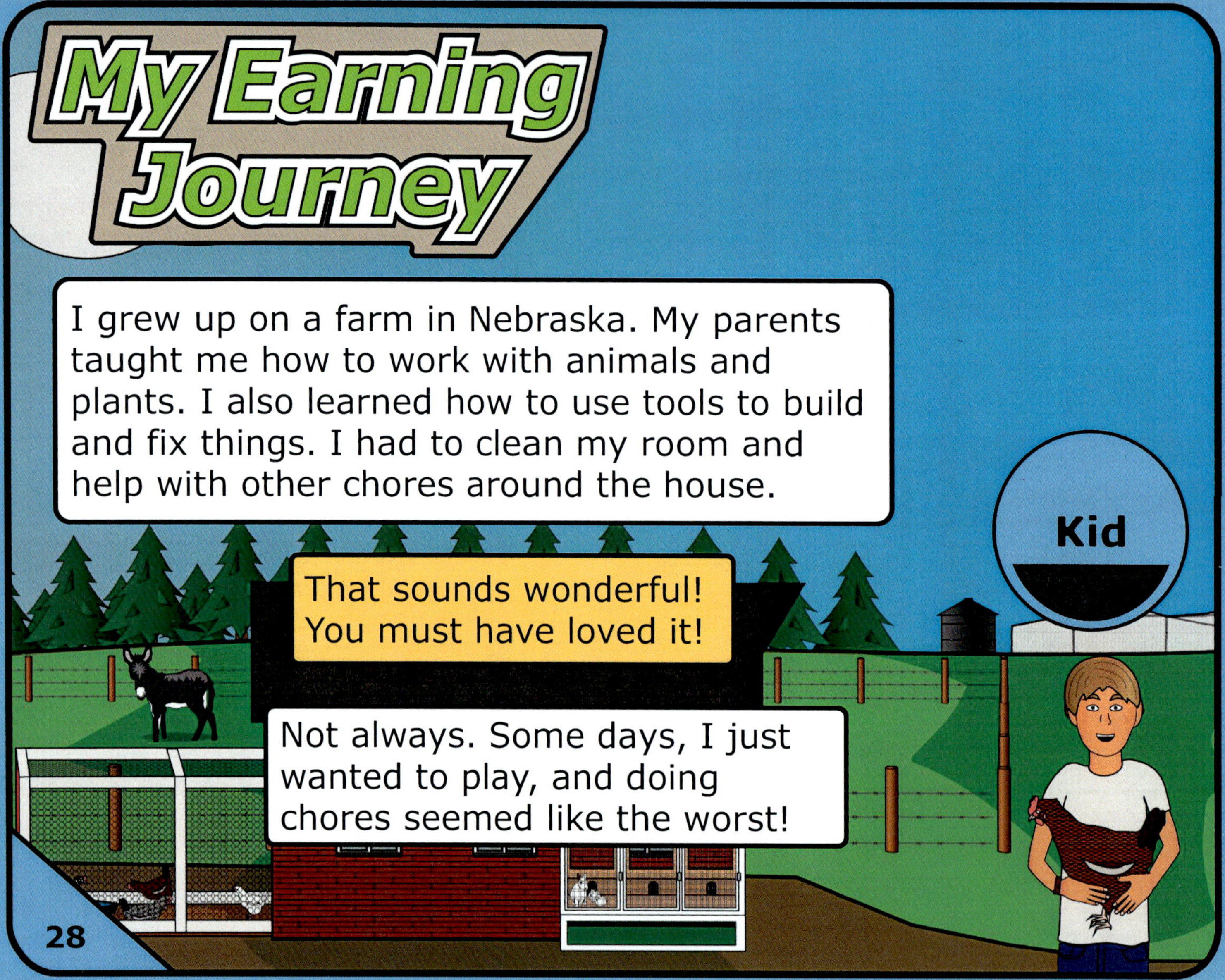
My Earning Journey
I grew up on a farm in Nebraska. My parents taught me how to work with animals and plants. I also learned how to use tools to build and fix things. I had to clean my room and help with other chores around the house.
Kid
That sounds wonderful! You must have loved it!
Not always. Some days, I just wanted to play, and doing chores seemed like the worst!

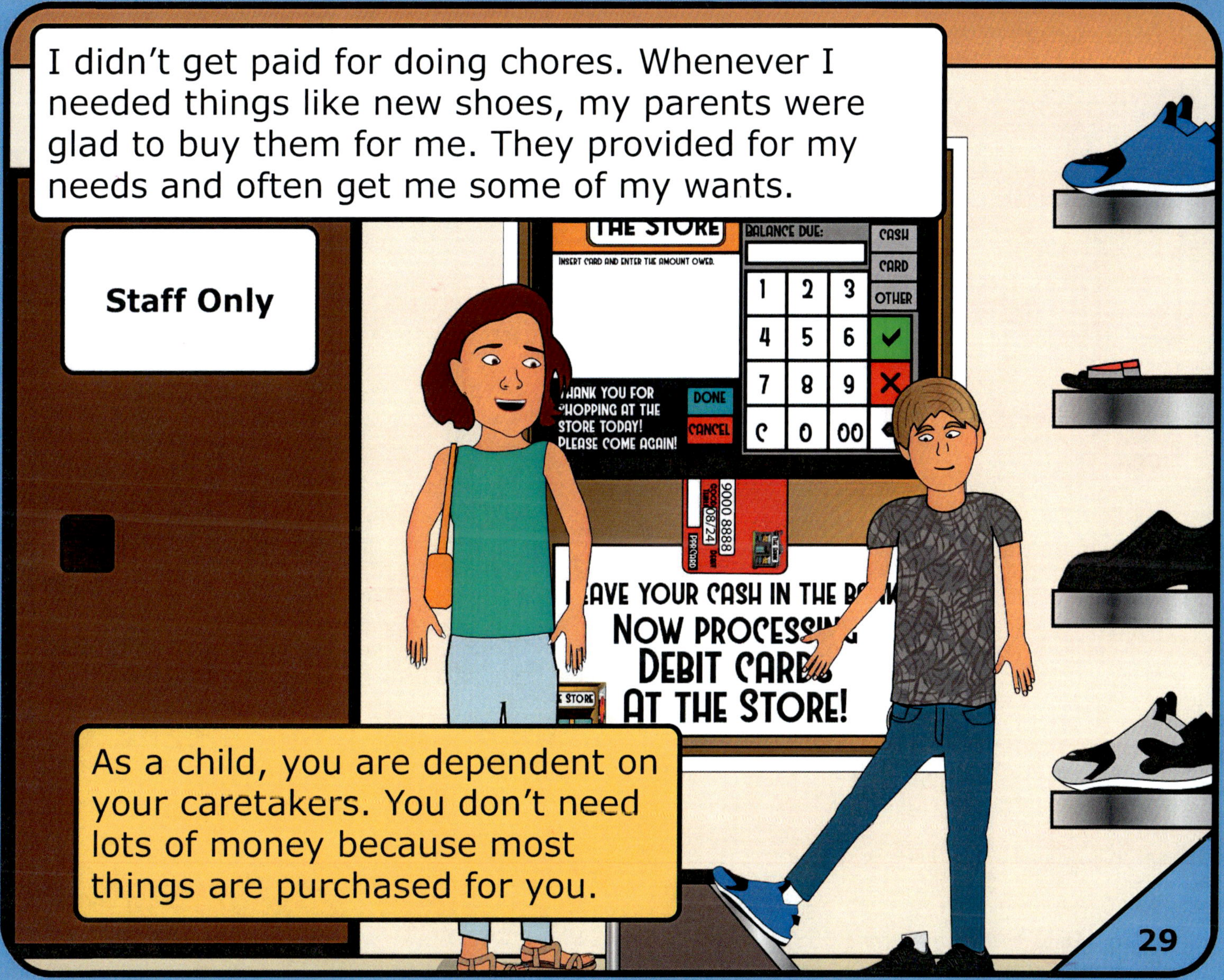
I didn't get paid for doing chores. Whenever I needed things like new shoes, my parents were glad to buy them for me. They provided for my needs and often get me some of my wants.
Staff Only
BALANCE DUE:
CASH
CARD
OTHER
INSERT CARD AND ENTER THE AMOUNT OWED.
DONE
CANCEL
STORE TODAY!
PLEASE COME AGAIN!
AT THE STORE!
As a child, you are dependent on your caretakers. You don't need lots of money because most things are purchased for you.

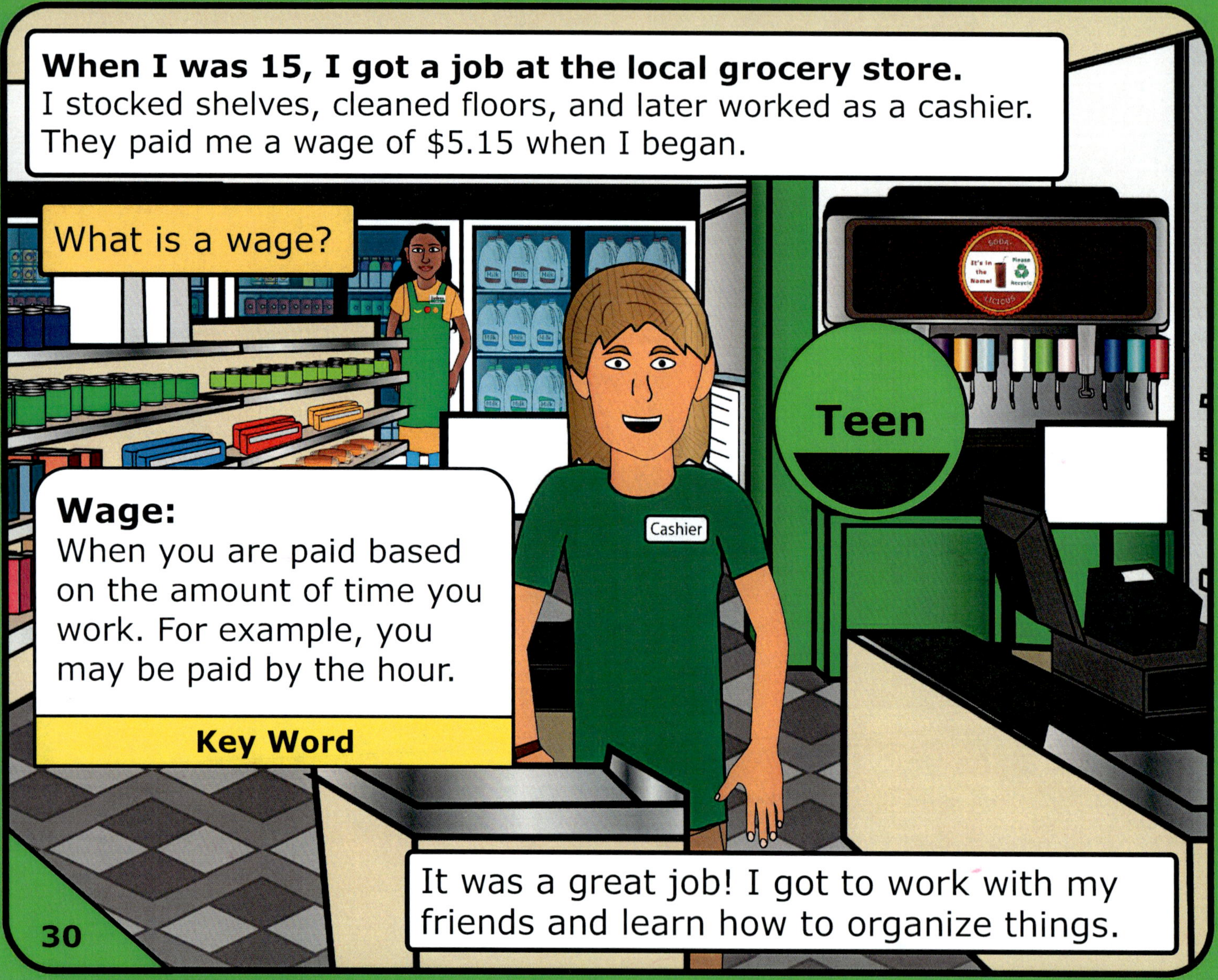
When I was 15, I got a job at the local grocery store.
I stocked shelves, cleaned floors, and later worked as a cashier. They paid me a wage of $5.15 when I began.
What is a wage?
Teen
Cashier
Wage:
When you are paid based on the amount of time you work. For example, you may be paid by the hour.
Key Word
It was a great job! I got to work with my friends and learn how to organize things.

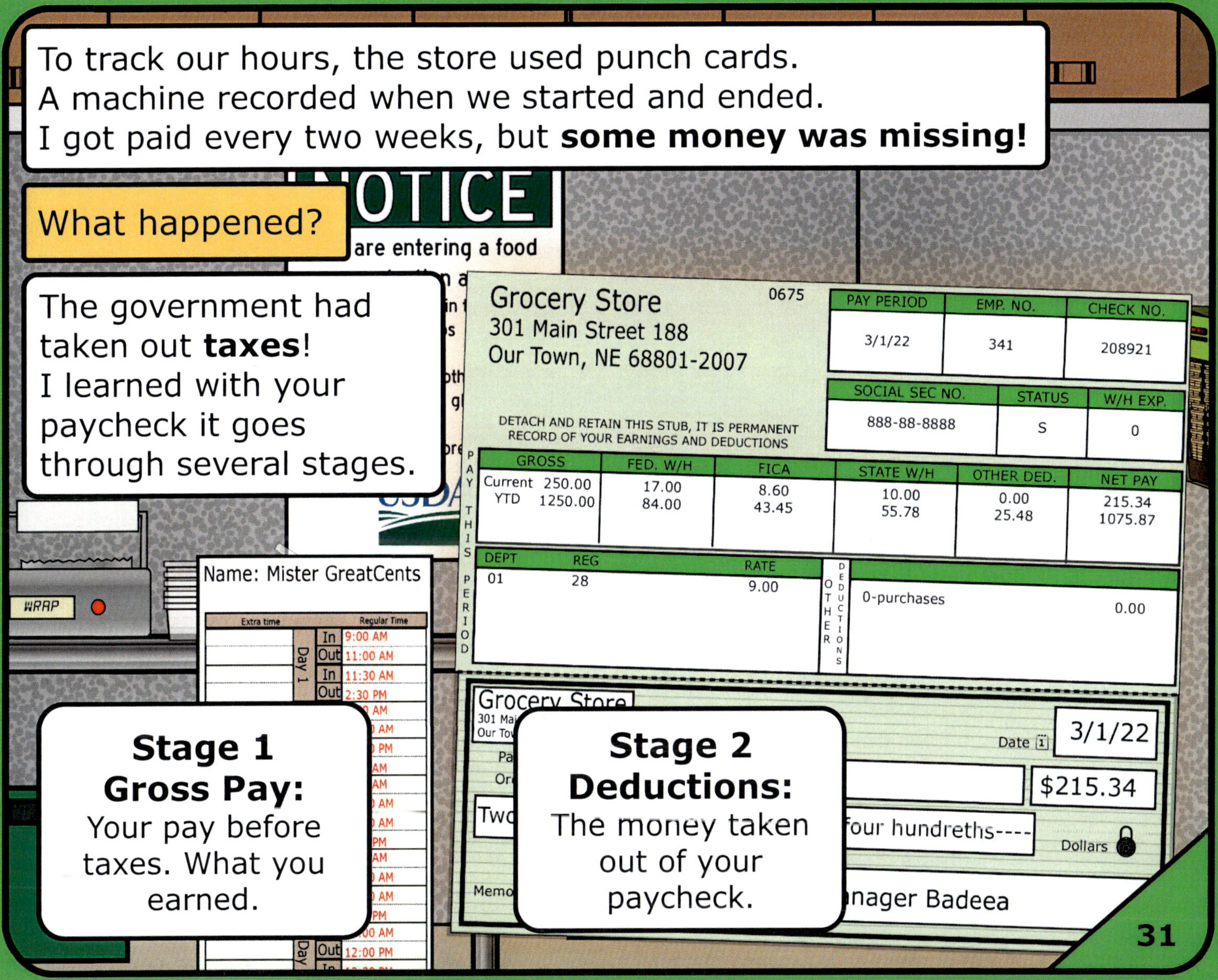
To track our hours, the store used punch cards.
A machine recorded when we started and ended.
I got paid every two weeks, but **some money was missing!**
What happened?
The government had taken out **taxes**! I learned with your paycheck it goes through several stages.
Grocery Store
301 Main Street 188
Our Town, NE 68801-2007
0675
PAY PERIOD 3/1/22
EMP. NO. 341
CHECK NO. 208921
SOCIAL SEC NO. 888-88-8888
STATUS S
W/H EXP. 0
DETACH AND RETAIN THIS STUB, IT IS PERMANENT RECORD OF YOUR EARNINGS AND DEDUCTIONS
PAY THIS PERIOD
GROSS Current 250.00 YTD 1250.00
FED. W/H 17.00 84.00
FICA 8.60 43.45
STATE W/H 10.00 55.78
OTHER DED. 0.00 25.48
NET PAY 215.34 1075.87
DEPT 01
REG 28
RATE 9.00
OTHER DEDUCTIONS
0-purchases 0.00
Name: Mister GreatCents
Extra time
Regular Time
Day 1
In 9:00 AM
Out 11:00 AM
In 11:30 AM
Out 2:30 PM
Out 12:00 PM
Date 3/1/22
$215.34
four hundreths----
Dollars
Memo
nager Badeea
Stage 1
Gross Pay:
Your pay before taxes. What you earned.
Stage 2
Deductions:
The money taken out of your paycheck.

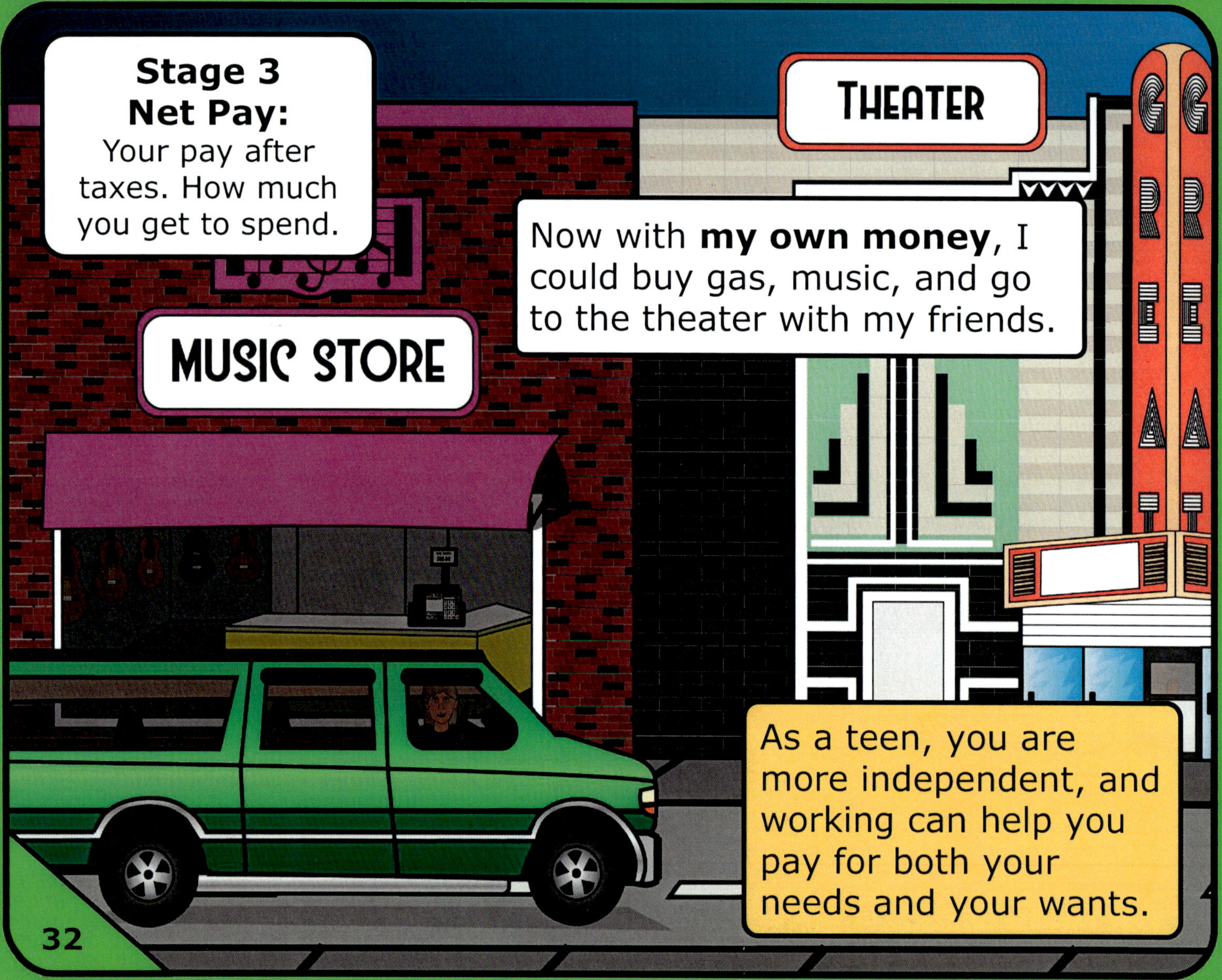
Stage 3
Net Pay:
Your pay after taxes. How much you get to spend.
THEATER
GREAT
Now with my own money, I could buy gas, music, and go to the theater with my friends.
MUSIC STORE
As a teen, you are more independent, and working can help you pay for both your needs and your wants.

After graduating from high school, I had to decide what my next steps would be. I had several options:

I could keep working at the grocery store. I would make money and could possibly get a raise, but I don't think I would like to do it long term.

I could join the military and defend my country. I would make money, gain experience, and learn skills. However, I didn't think this was the right choice for me.

I chose to go to college to continue my education.
I loved music and wanted a career as a radio host. College was my next step!

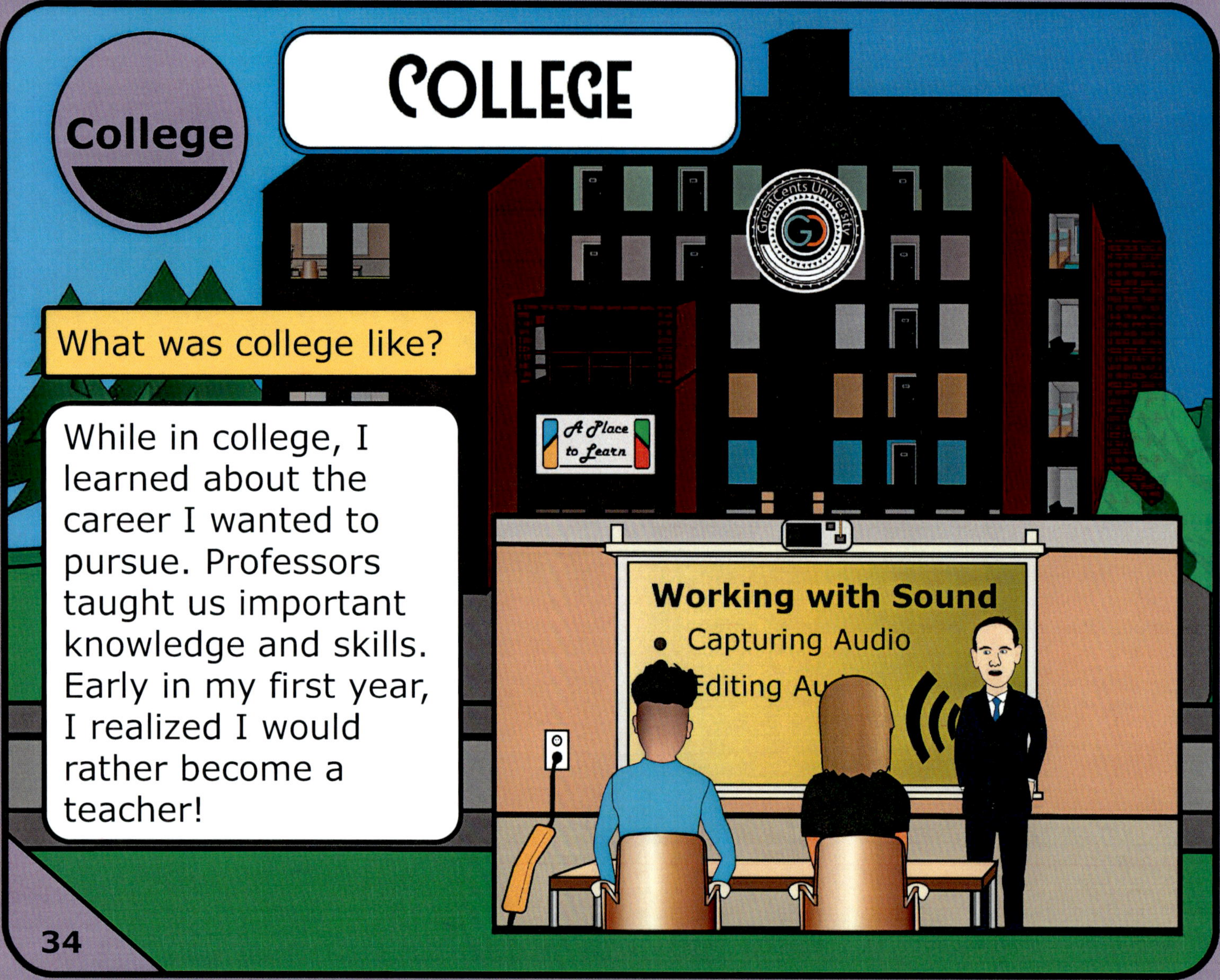
College
COLLEGE
GreatCents University
A Place to Learn
What was college like?
While in college, I learned about the career I wanted to pursue. Professors taught us important knowledge and skills. Early in my first year, I realized I would rather become a teacher!
Working with Sound
Capturing Audio
Editing Au

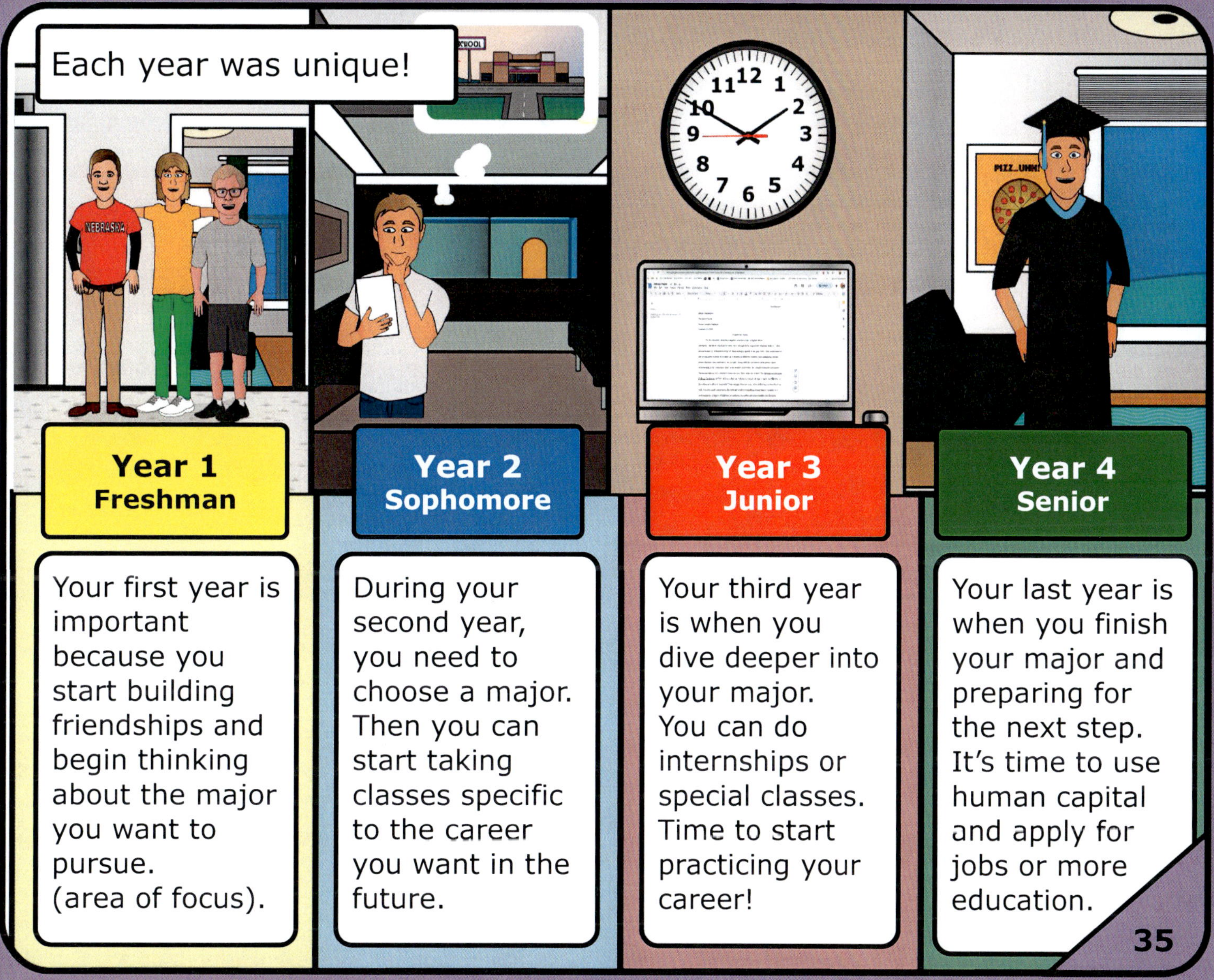
Each year was unique!
Year 1
Freshman
Your first year is important because you start building friendships and begin thinking about the major you want to pursue. (area of focus).
Year 2
Sophomore
During your second year, you need to choose a major. Then you can start taking classes specific to the career you want in the future.
Year 3
Junior
Your third year is when you dive deeper into your major. You can do internships or special classes. Time to start practicing your career!
Year 4
Senior
Your last year is when you finish your major and preparing for the next step. It's time to use human capital and apply for jobs or more education.
NEBRASKA

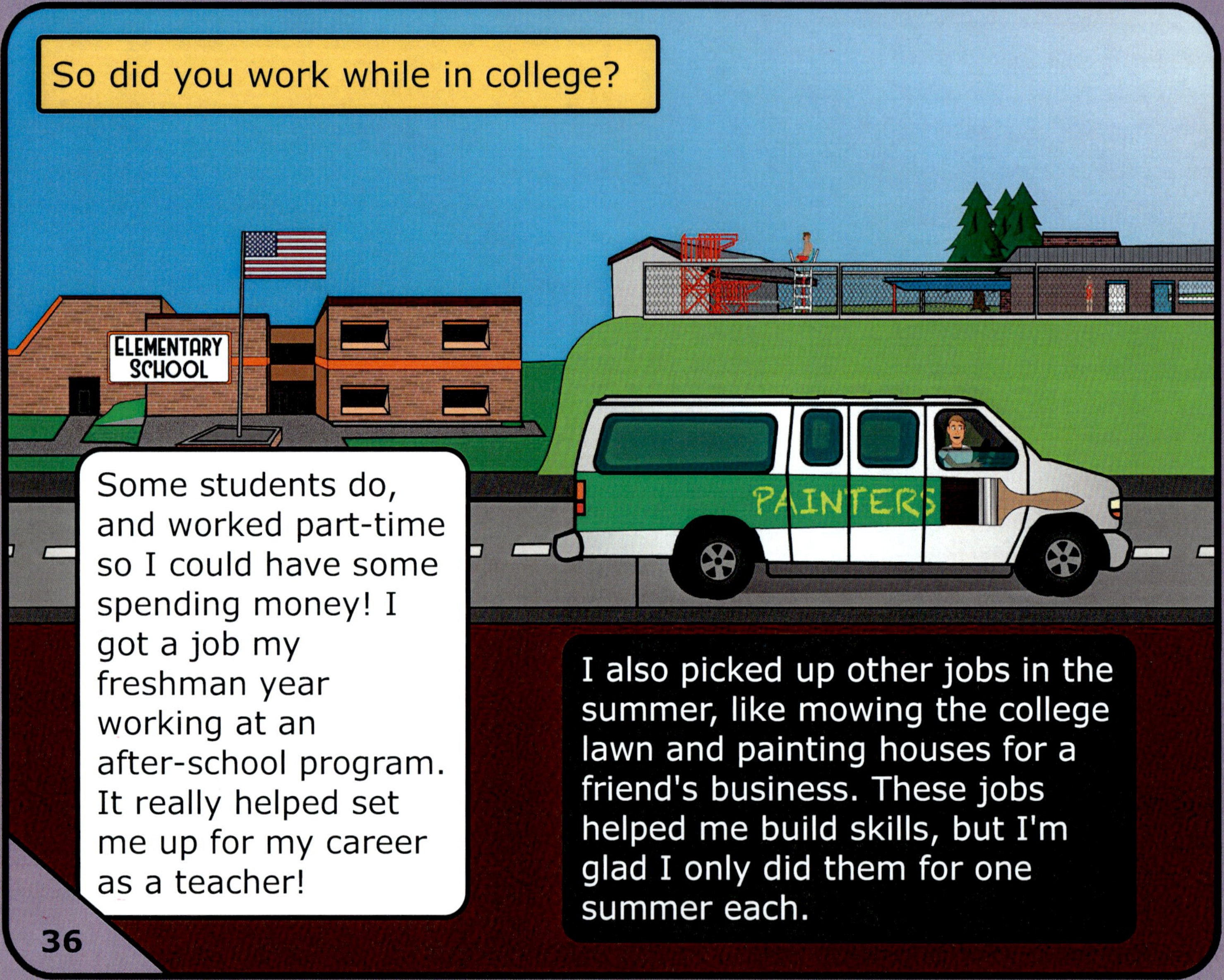
So did you work while in college?
ELEMENTARY SCHOOL
Some students do, and worked part-time so I could have some spending money! I got a job my freshman year working at an after-school program. It really helped set me up for my career as a teacher!
PAINTERS
I also picked up other jobs in the summer, like mowing the college lawn and painting houses for a friend's business. These jobs helped me build skills, but I'm glad I only did them for one summer each.

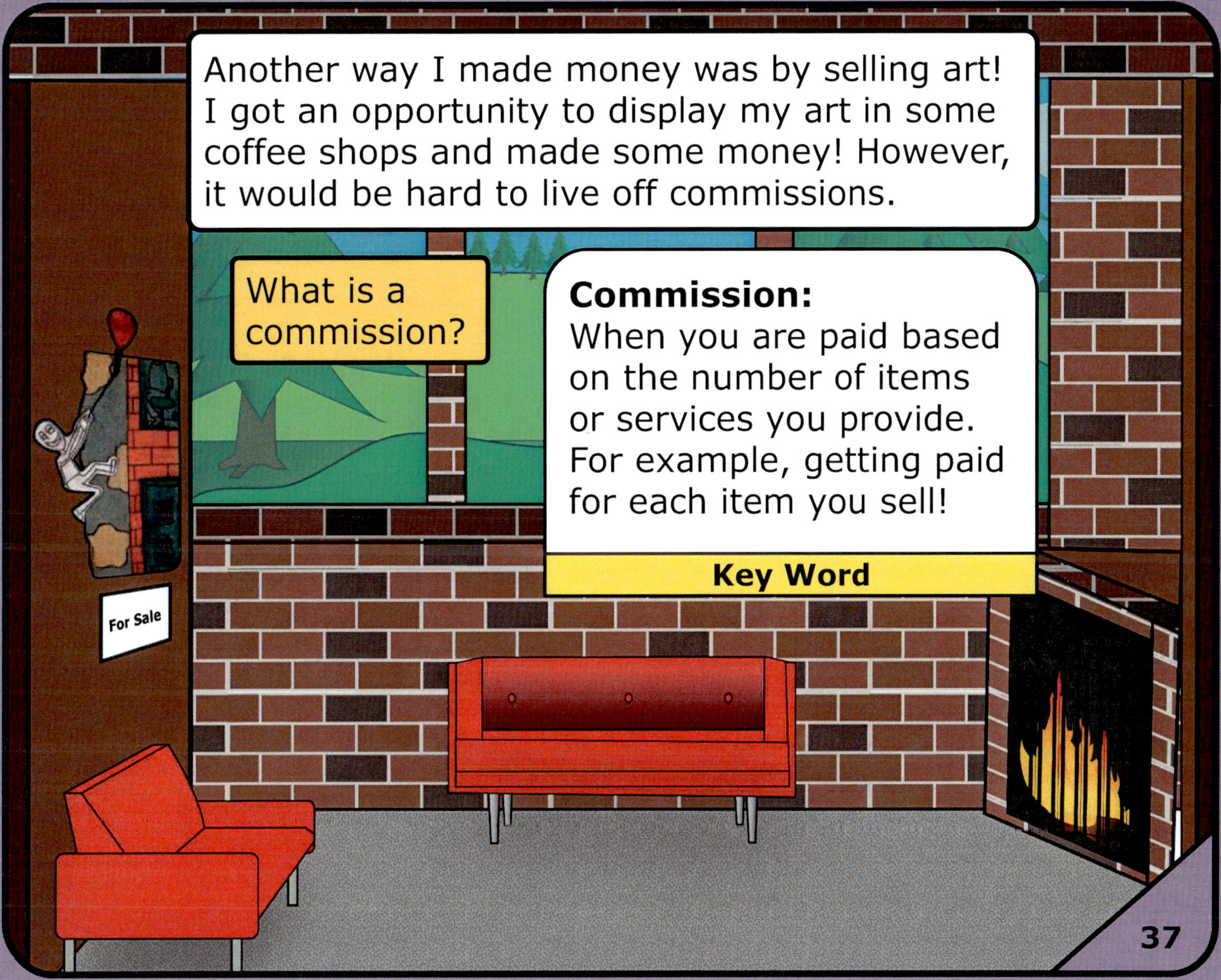

Another way I made money was by selling art! I got an opportunity to display my art in some coffee shops and made some money! However, it would be hard to live off commissions.
What is a commission?
Commission:
When you are paid based on the number of items or services you provide. For example, getting paid for each item you sell!
Key Word
For Sale

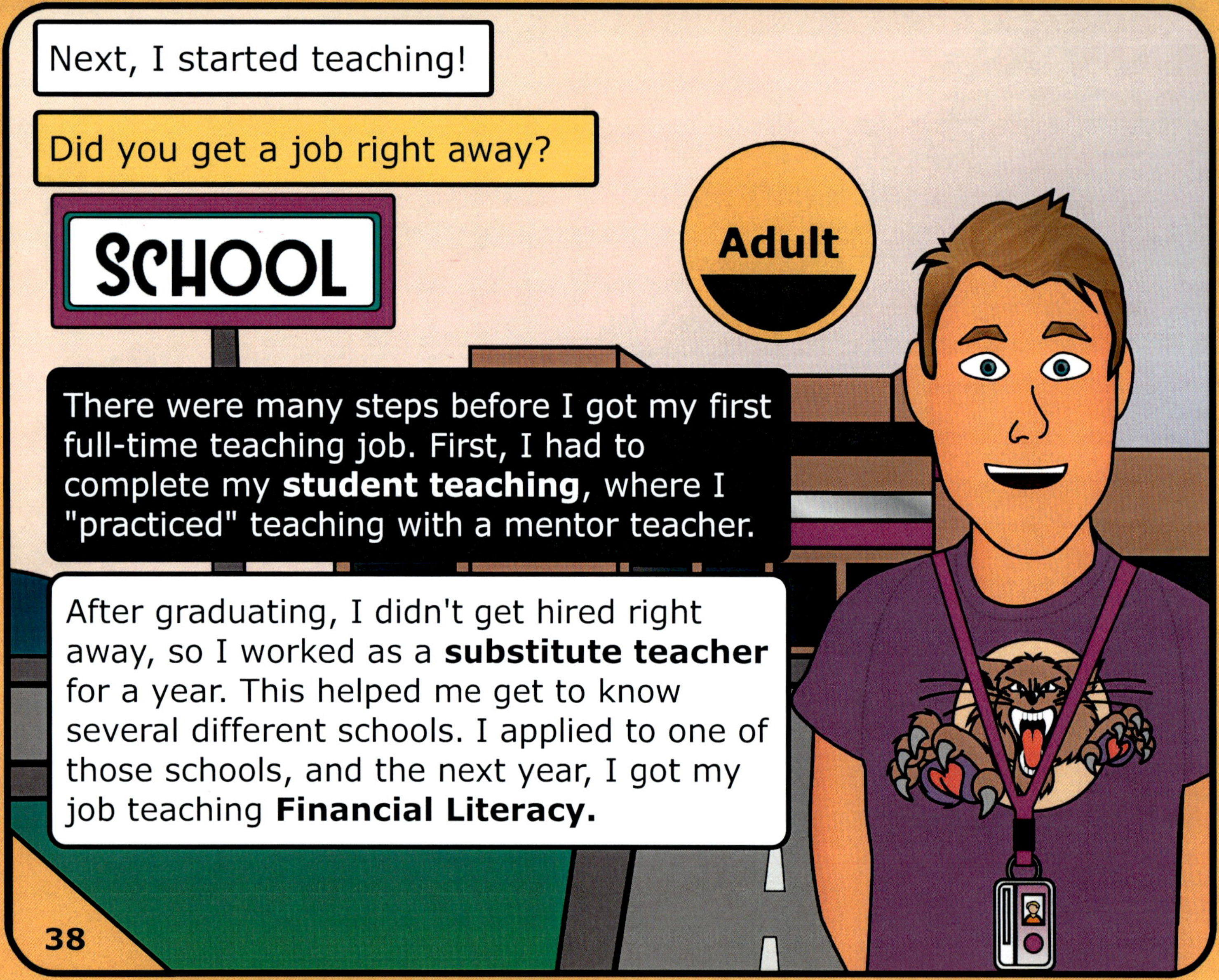
Next, I started teaching!
Did you get a job right away?
SCHOOL
Adult
There were many steps before I got my first full-time teaching job. First, I had to complete my **student teaching**, where I "practiced" teaching with a mentor teacher.
After graduating, I didn't get hired right away, so I worked as a **substitute teacher** for a year. This helped me get to know several different schools. I applied to one of those schools, and the next year, I got my job teaching **Financial Literacy.**

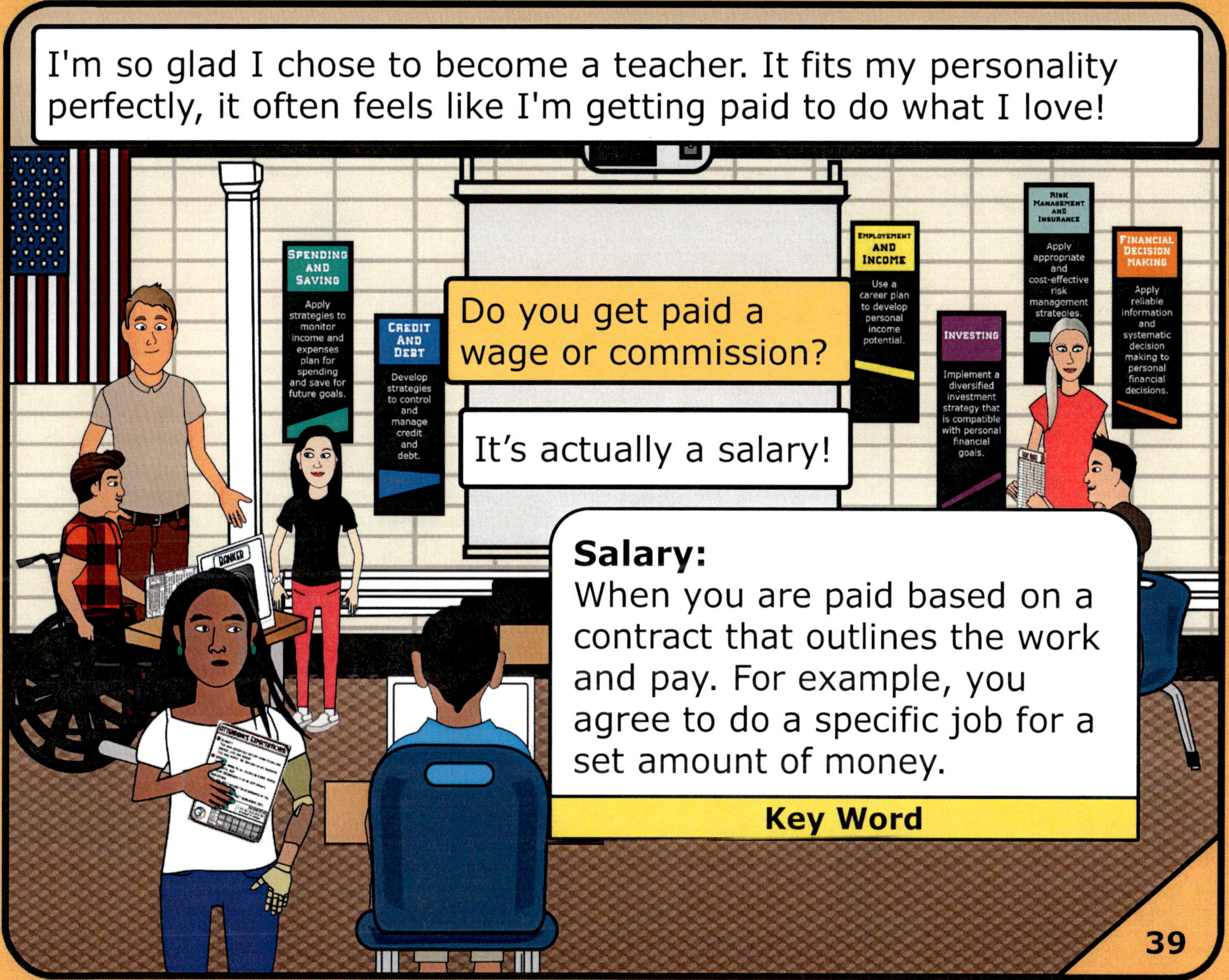
I'm so glad I chose to become a teacher. It fits my personality perfectly, it often feels like I'm getting paid to do what I love!
Spending and Saving
Apply strategies to monitor income and expenses plan for spending and save for future goals.
Credit and Debt
Develop strategies to control and manage credit and debt.
Employment and Income
Use a career plan to develop personal income potential.
Investing
Implement a diversified investment strategy that is compatible with personal financial goals.
Risk Management and Insurance
Apply appropriate and cost-effective risk management strategies.
Financial Decision Making
Apply reliable information and systematic decision making to personal financial decisions.
Do you get paid a wage or commission?
It's actually a salary!
Salary:
When you are paid based on a contract that outlines the work and pay. For example, you agree to do a specific job for a set amount of money.
Key Word

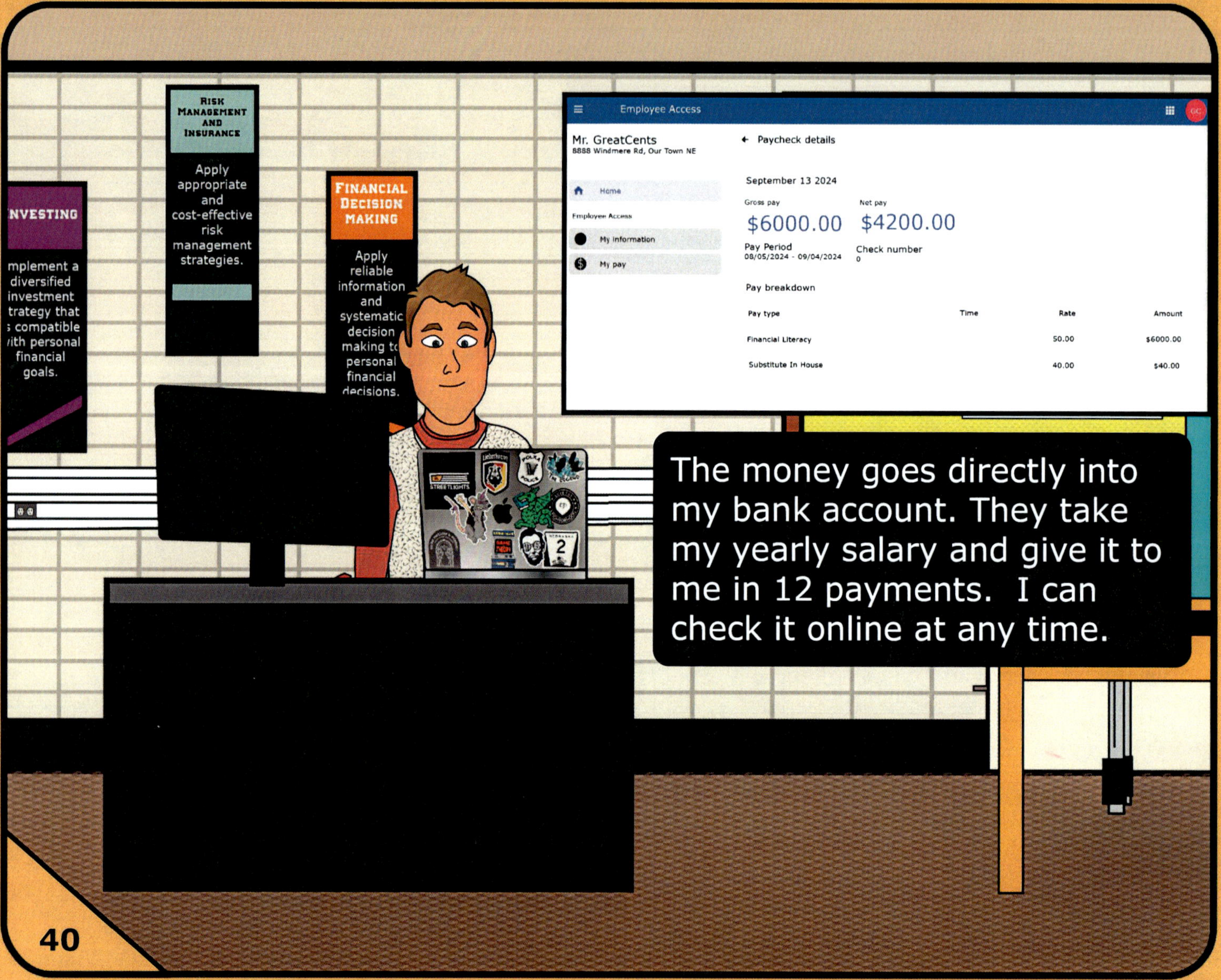
RISK MANAGEMENT AND INSURANCE
Apply appropriate and cost-effective risk management strategies.
FINANCIAL DECISION MAKING
Apply reliable information and systematic decision making to personal financial decisions.
Employee Access
Mr. GreatCents
8888 Windmere Rd, Our Town NE
Paycheck details
Home
Employee Access
My information
My pay
September 13 2024
Gross pay
$6000.00
Net pay
$4200.00
Pay Period
08/05/2024 - 09/04/2024
Check number
0
Pay breakdown
Pay type
Time
Rate
Amount
Financial Literacy
50.00
$6000.00
Substitute In House
40.00
$40.00
The money goes directly into my bank account. They take my yearly salary and give it to me in 12 payments. I can check it online at any time.

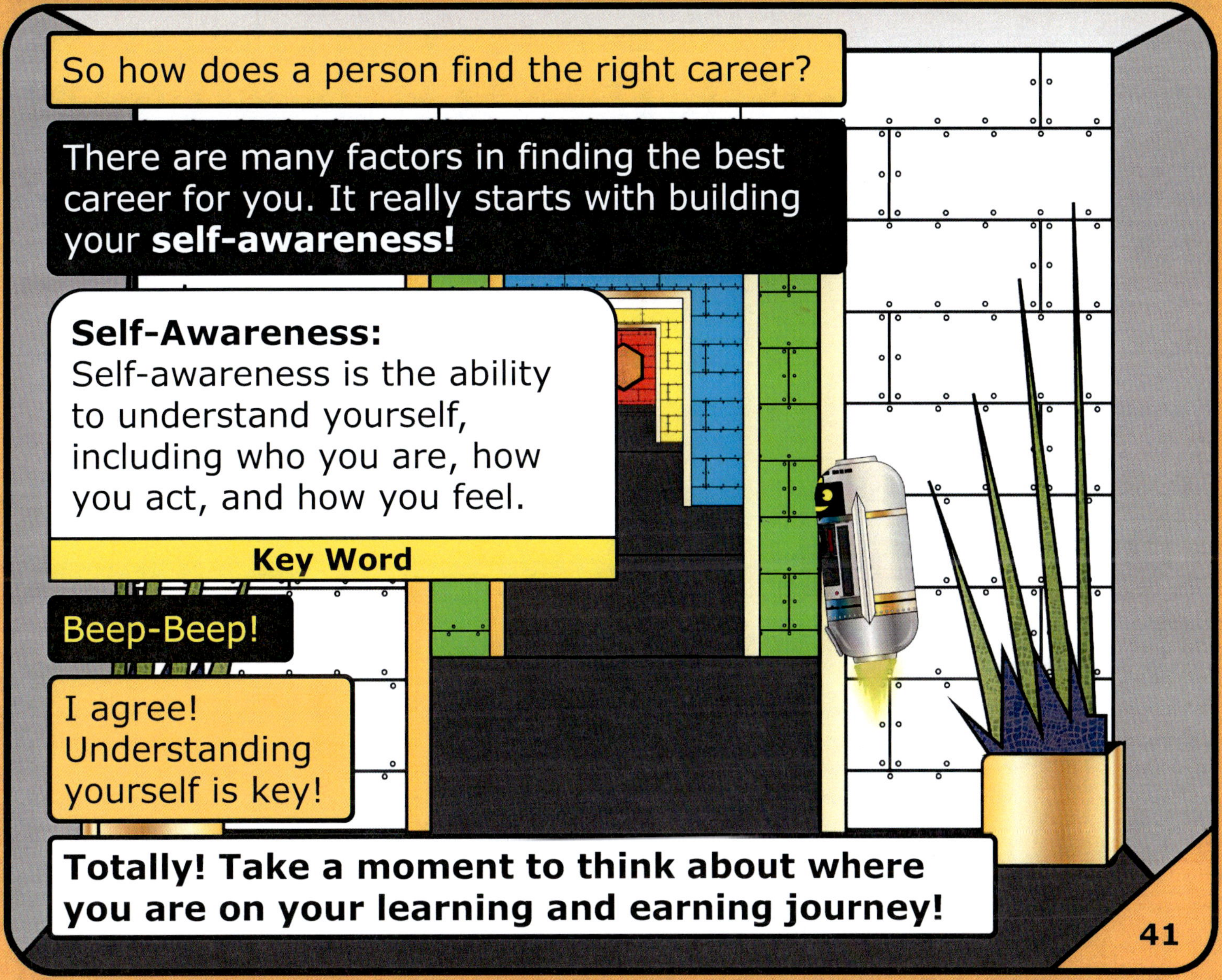
So how does a person find the right career?
There are many factors in finding the best career for you. It really starts with building your **self-awareness!**
Self-Awareness: Self-awareness is the ability to understand yourself, including who you are, how you act, and how you feel.
Key Word
Beep-Beep!
I agree! Understanding yourself is key!
Totally! Take a moment to think about where you are on your learning and earning journey!

What has your earning journey looked like so far?

Kid

Who took care of you when you were little?

Describe your first memories of money:

Teen

How would earning money as a teen give a person more freedom?

What are some jobs that you would be interested in?

Next Step

After you graduate from high school what do you think will be your next step?

☐ ☐ ☐

What do you think this will this look like?

Beep-Beep!

Your Earning Journey

Adult

If you could have any career what would it be?

Who is someone that could guide you on your earning journey? Why?

What has their earning journey looked like?

Step 1:
Describe a person's earning journey.

1

Next task: Water the plants. Get ready to see some unique and wild flowers! Each one was grown from a seed and has had its own journey of growth. They were planted by Beatrix, who has a green thumb, meaning she's very good with plants!

To build our self-awareness, we're first going to explore our **"Who."** **By doing this it will help us make sense of** our **identity**!
Identity: (Who):
Identity is who you are and how you see yourself. It shapes the way you understand the world around you.
Key Word

M.A.X
Who am I?
That’s a deep question, and answering it requires some wisdom. One of the most important factors in how we feel about ourselves is what we believe about ourselves and **“our story.”**

In our last journey, *How to Handle Risk and Stress*, we discussed how our **thoughts**, **feelings**, and **behaviors** are connected. We call it our **TFB** and through **self management** we can make confident choices!

I read the book **How to Handle Risk and Stress** in 1.6 seconds and it was amazing! I bet this **self-awareness** will help us understand ourselves even better!

Having a clear view of our **identity** will help us make better decisions in all areas of life!

If you're just jumping in, here's a quick recap and connection!

Our Thoughts:
What you think about or focus on affects your feelings.
Knowing who you are gives you a solid foundation for your choices!

Our Feelings:
Happiness, fear, sadness, anger, disgust, and surprise all come from your thoughts. A true view of yourself helps you **stay balanced!**

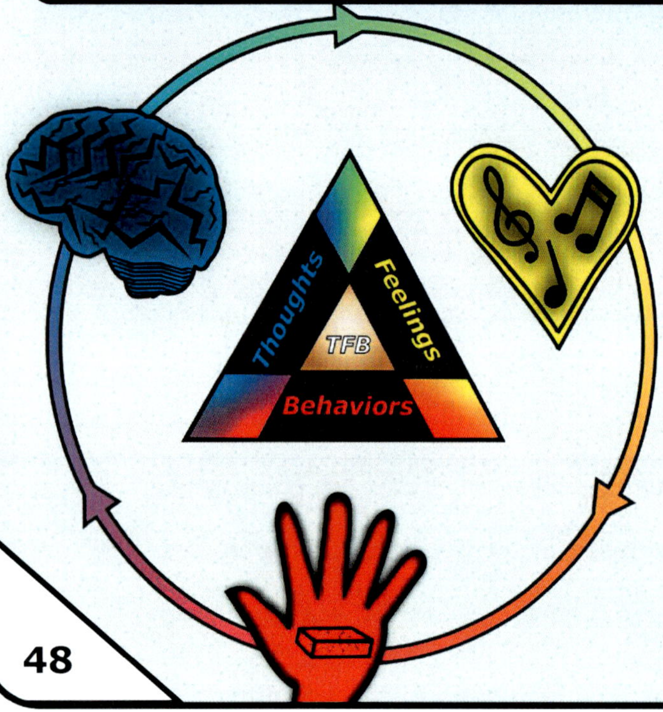

Our Behavior:
The way you act comes from our thoughts and feelings. Recognizing your background and experiences can **help you understand your behavior.**

Our Lives:
This process of understanding your inner world can help you **enjoy life more** and succeed in finding jobs and careers!

Who do you listen to?

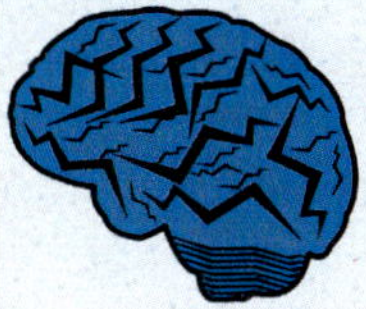

Thoughts: Who are several people that you trust? Why?

Their words are important in shaping your view of yourself.

Feelings: If someone tells you that they are proud of you how would that make you feel? Why?

What we believe shapes our feelings.

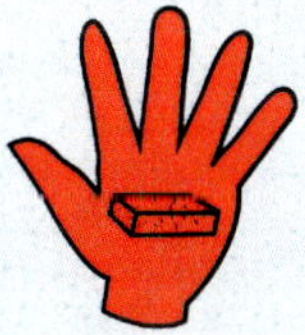

Behaviors: How do your actions show what you believe about yourself? Give an example!

Our actions show what believe and value.

Today's Movie:
Identity!
POPCORN
Let's take a small detour to better understand identity. This is the base's mini theater, but… I don't think that popcorn is fresh!
It was three months ago!

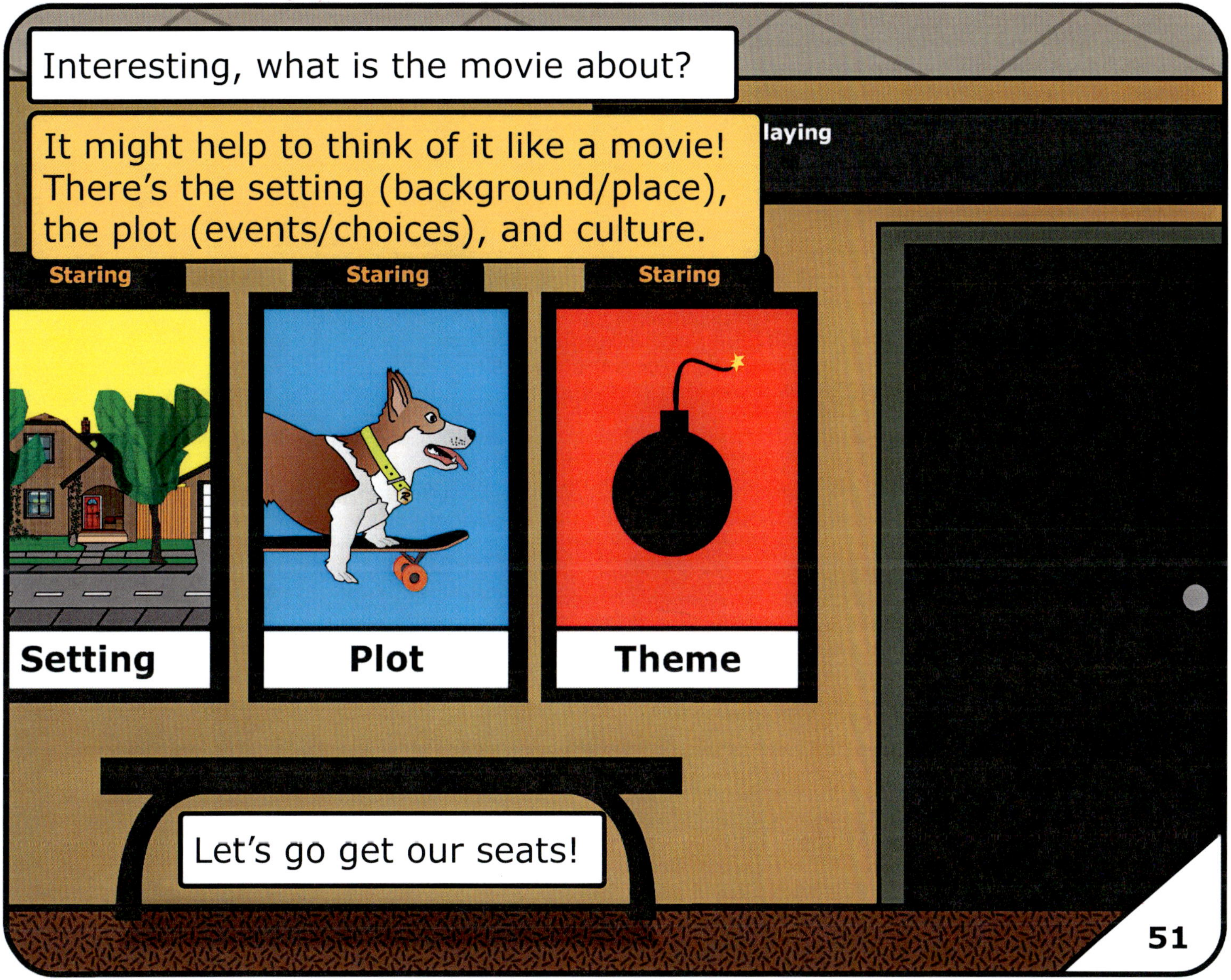
Interesting, what is the movie about?
It might help to think of it like a movie! There's the setting (background/place), the plot (events/choices), and culture.
laying
Staring
Staring
Staring
Setting
Plot
Theme
Let's go get our seats!

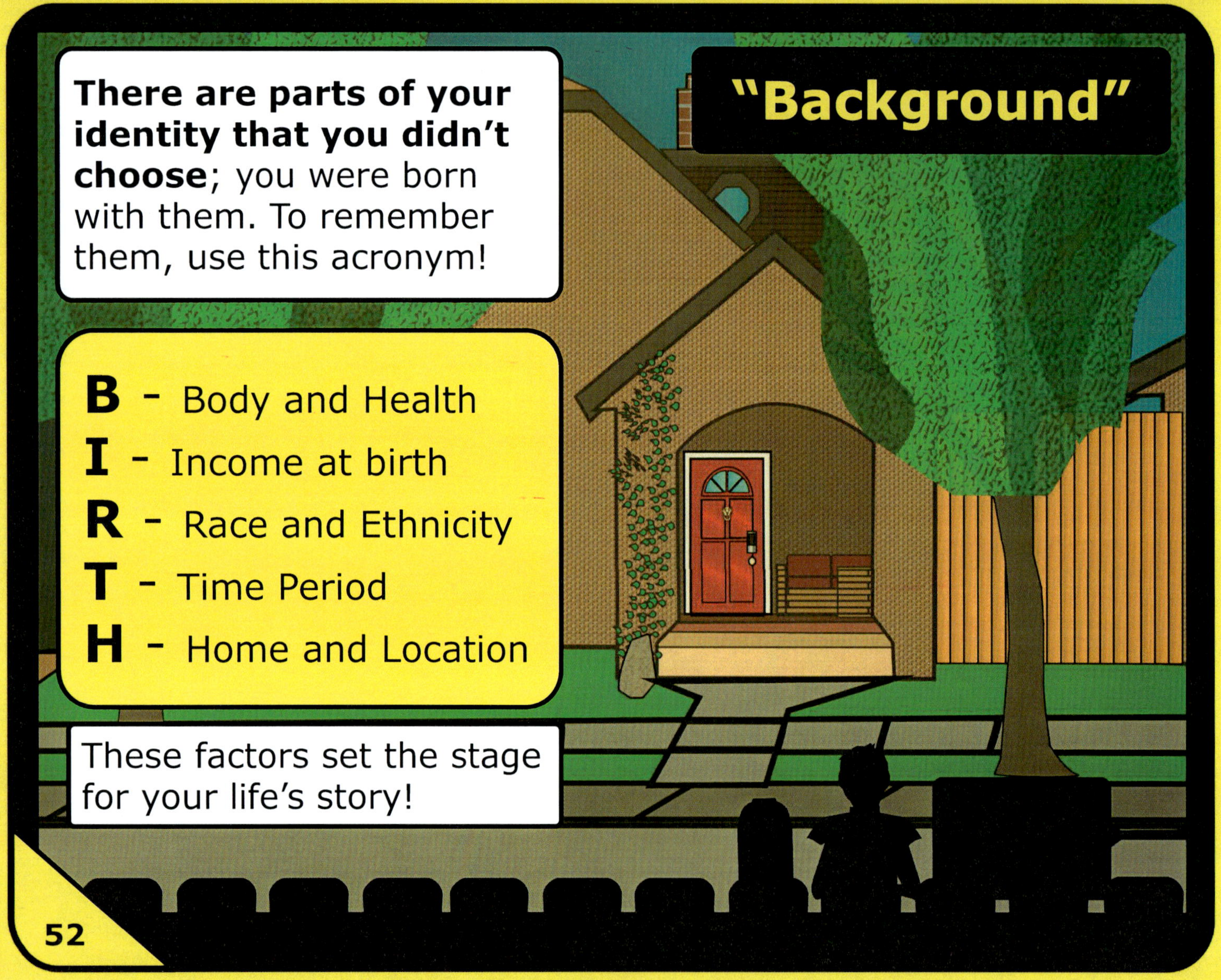
"Background"
There are parts of your identity that you didn't choose; you were born with them. To remember them, use this acronym!
B - Body and Health
I - Income at birth
R - Race and Ethnicity
T - Time Period
H - Home and Location
These factors set the stage for your life's story!

You don't get a choice when it comes to:

Your Body & Health

The body you were born into:
- Body Type
- Health
- Genetics
- Disabilities

Your Income At Birth

Your financial background when you were born:
- Poverty
- Middle Class
- Wealth

Your Race & Ethnicity

Your unique physical features the background of your family:
- Ancestry
- Skin color
- Traditions
- Challenges

Your Time Period

The year you were born into and world events that are happening:
- Historical Events
- Technology
- Opportunities

Your Home & Location

How your family is structured and where you live:
- Who is raising you
- Urban - city
- Rural - small town
- Suburban
- Resources

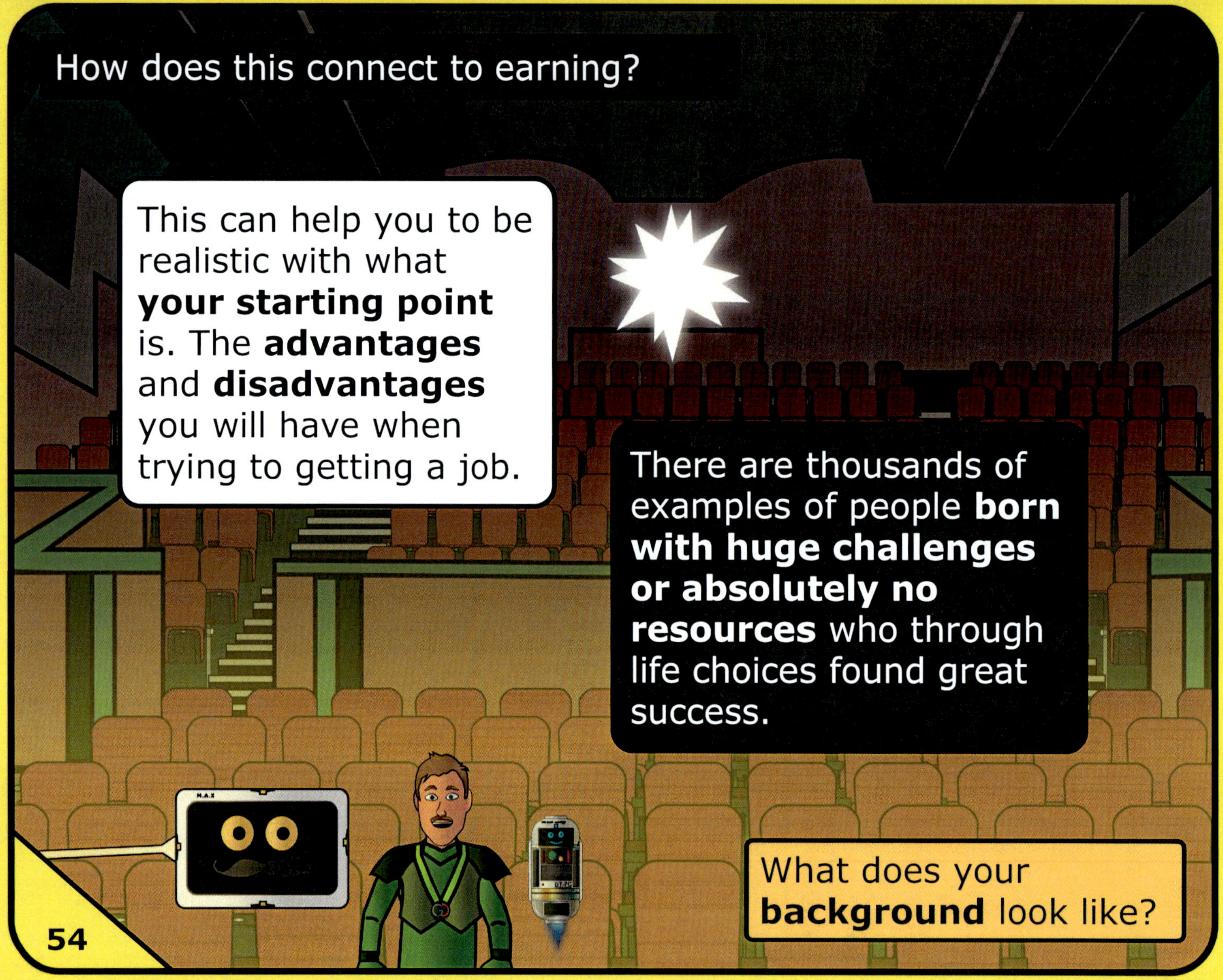
How does this connect to earning?
This can help you to be realistic with what **your starting point** is. The **advantages** and **disadvantages** you will have when trying to getting a job.
There are thousands of examples of people **born with huge challenges or absolutely no resources** who through life choices found great success.
What does your **background** look like?
M.A.X

Your Body & Health

What are some habits you can build to take care of your body and mind?	

Your Income At Birth

How does a families budget shape their children's opportunities? Why?	

Your Race & Ethnicity

How does your race, culture or ethnicity shape who you are?	

Your Time Period

Share a new technology that is being used today. How does it affect you?	

Your Home & Location

Do you live in a rural, urban or suburban area? How does that shape your identity?	

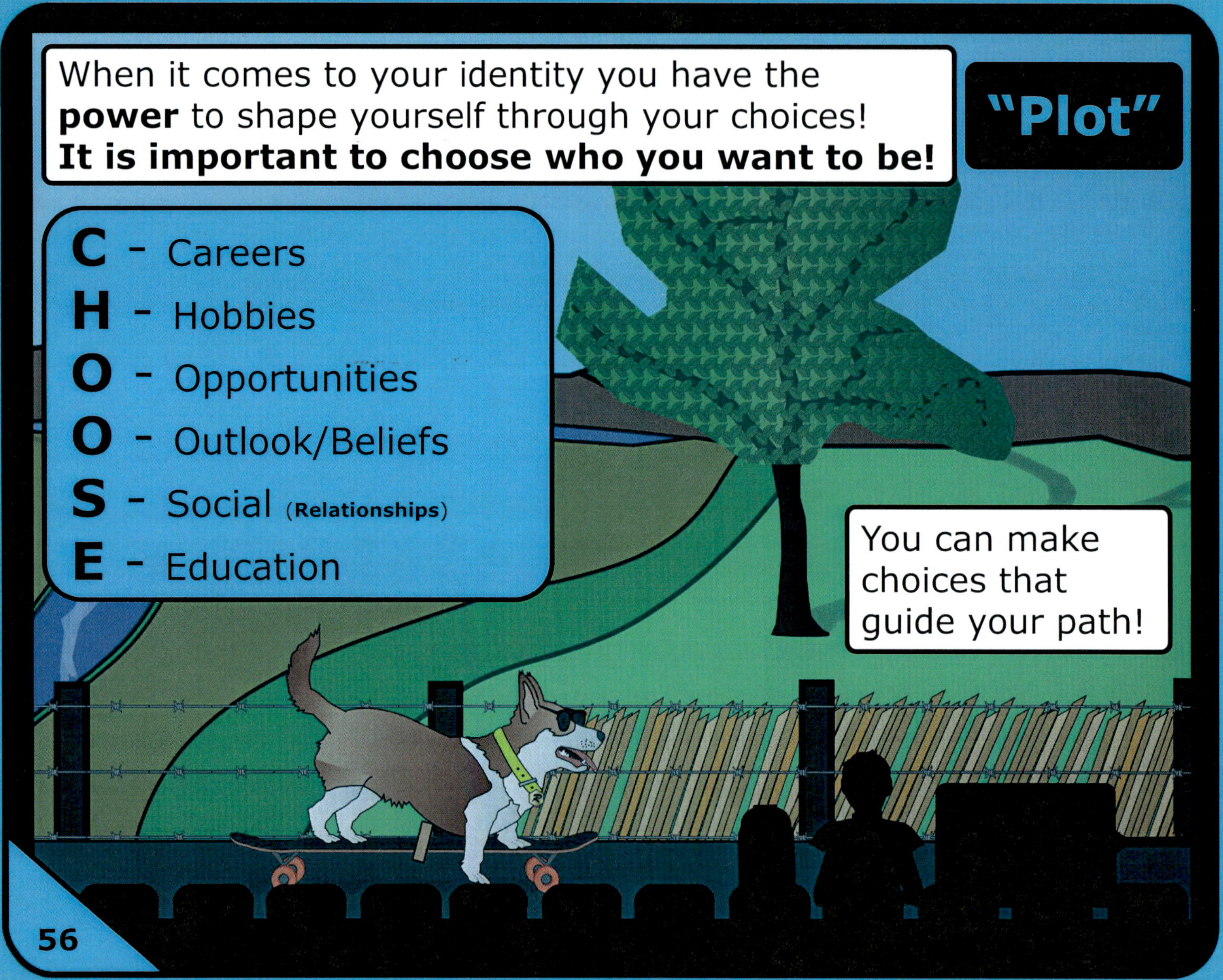
When it comes to your identity you have the **power** to shape yourself through your choices! **It is important to choose who you want to be!**
"Plot"
C - Careers
H - Hobbies
O - Opportunities
O - Outlook/Beliefs
S - Social (Relationships)
E - Education
You can make choices that guide your path!

Your Career

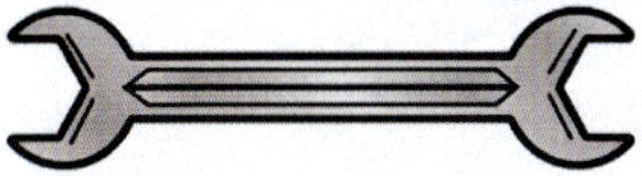

Your career will shape much of your life:

- Your money
- Your time
- Your knowledge
- Your Skills

Your Hobbies

How you spend your free time is important:

- It bringing positivity into your life
- It helps you to connect you with others

Your Opportunities

When you have the chance to do something special:

- Making memories
- Build self-confidence
- See the world

Your Outlooks (Beliefs)

How you understand the world affects how you see yourself:

- Your beliefs on what is right and wrong
- Your place in the universe as you
- Religion/Faith/None

Your Social (Relationships)

You pick your friends and they help shape who you:

- The things you find interesting
- How you act toward other people
- Goals in life

Your Education (Intelligence)

Being a lifelong learner pays:

- The effort to grow as you learn
- The classes you choose to take
- Your job or career!

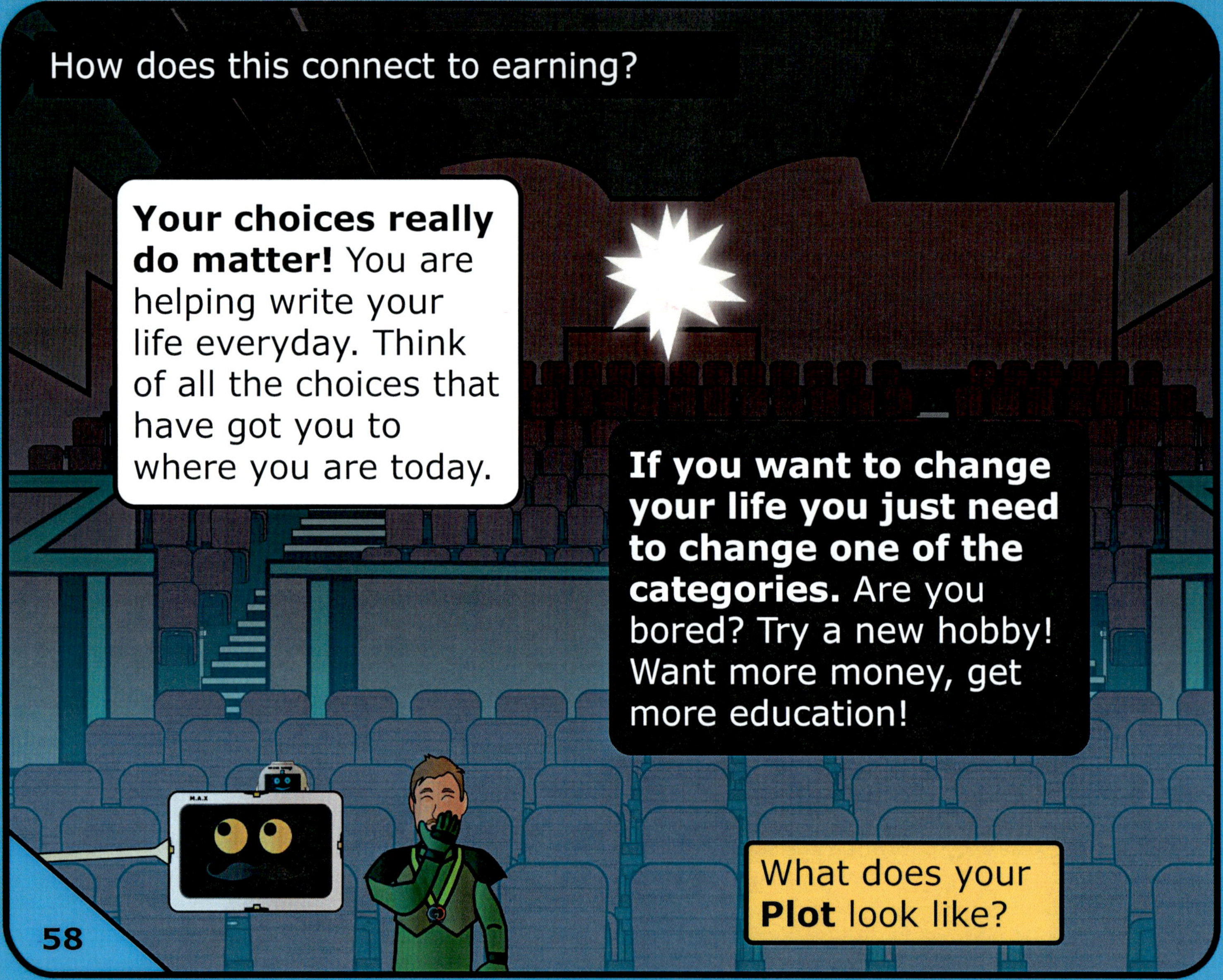

How does this connect to earning?
Your choices really do matter! You are helping write your life everyday. Think of all the choices that have got you to where you are today.
If you want to change your life you just need to change one of the categories. Are you bored? Try a new hobby! Want more money, get more education!
M.A.X
What does your **Plot** look like?

Your Career

Think of an adult you know that has a career. What skills do they need for that career?	

Your Hobbies

What are 3 hobbies that you enjoy doing?			

Your Opportunities

What are 2 cool opportunities you could do at your age?		

Your Outlooks (Beliefs)

How do your beliefs shape the way you treat others? Why?	

Your Social (Relationships)

Who are some of your closest friends? Why?	

Your Education (Intelligence)

What is a topic you enjoy learning about?	

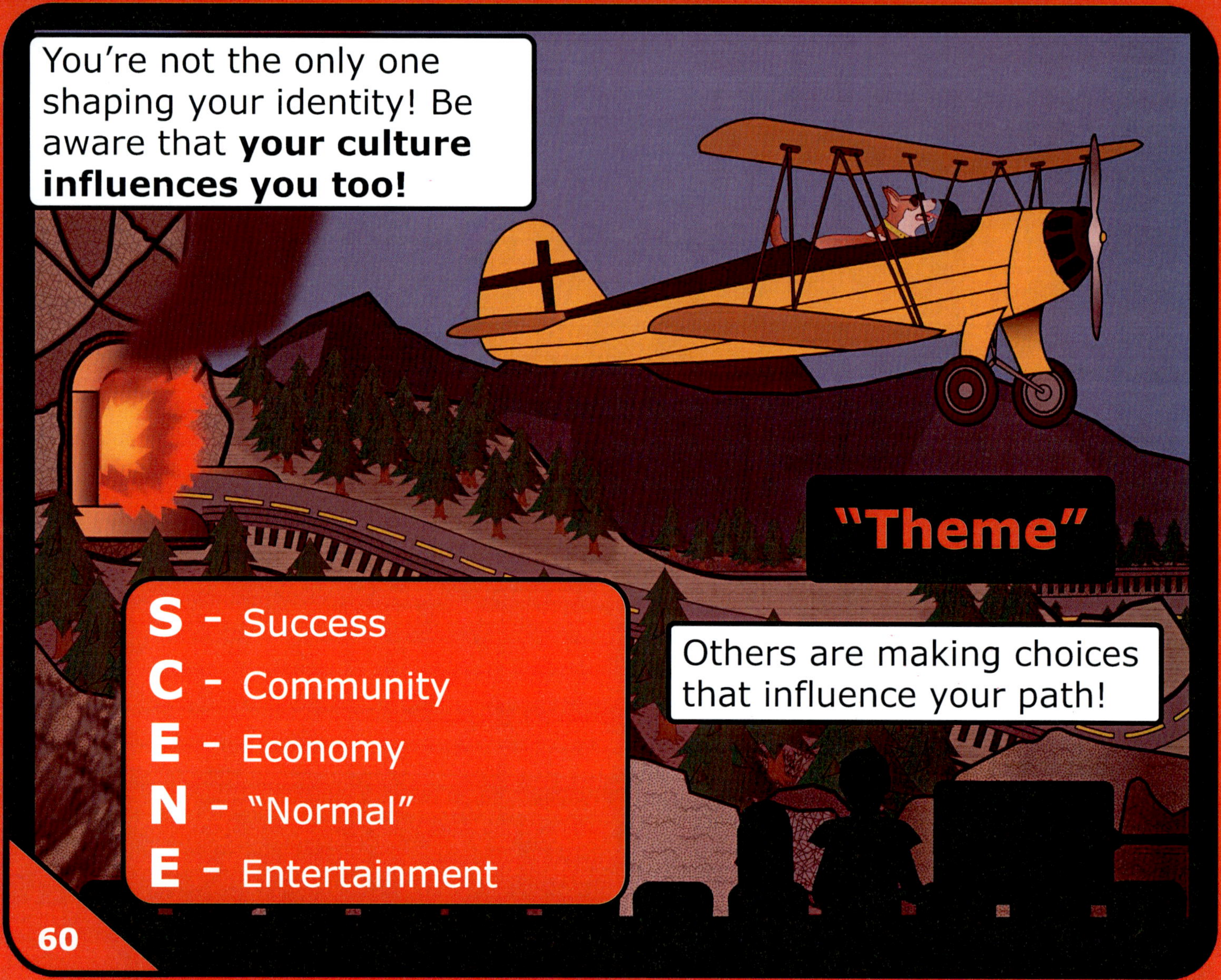
You're not the only one shaping your identity! Be aware that **your culture influences you too!**
"Theme"
S - Success
C - Community
E - Economy
N - "Normal"
E - Entertainment
Others are making choices that influence your path!

What Is "Success"

Culture great shapes our view of **what makes us successful**:

- Family • Friends • Faith
- Education • Sports • Fun
- Fitness • Freedom • Pay
- Adventure • Creativity

These are all great things, as long as you don't overdo it!

Your Entertainment

Culture through **social media, film, music, art** and **books** greatly shapes the way we see:

- Humor • Beauty • Character
- Priorities • Fame • Finances
- Family • Others • Violence

The things you let into your mind build your unique view.

Your Community

Your family and the people that you live around are a big part of shaping how you view yourself. **Having trusted adults who will protect you and encourage you** is huge part of building a healthy identity.

What Is "Normal"

Culture can shape how you view what is "normal":

- The said and unsaid "rules."
- What you should wear or do for fun.
- How you see yourself fitting into the your community.

Your Economy

Culture shapes how we view our money:

- If the economy is doing **poorly** people tend to **more careful** and **save more** money.
- If the economy is doing **well** people tend to **spend more** money.

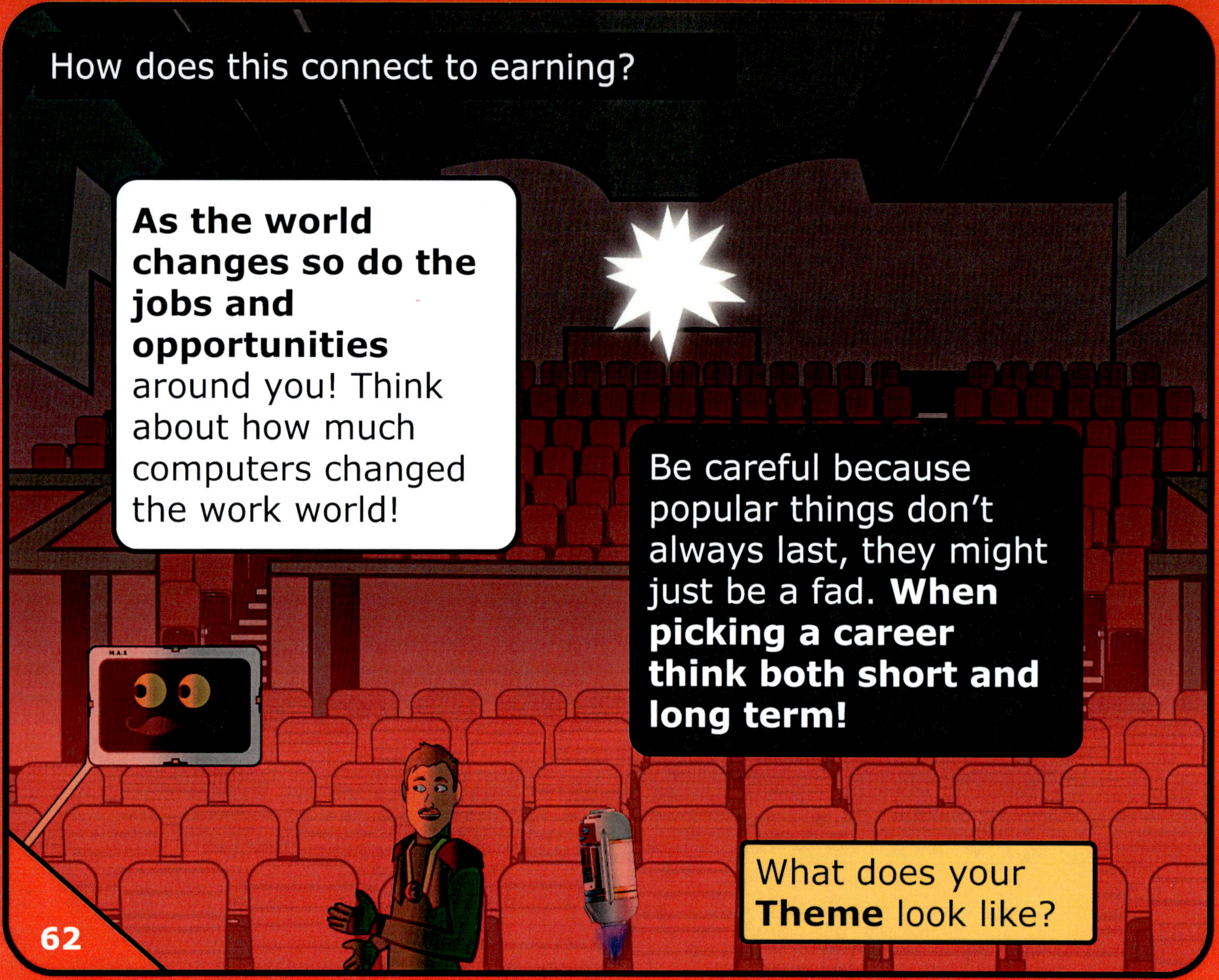
How does this connect to earning?
As the world changes so do the jobs and opportunities around you! Think about how much computers changed the work world!
Be careful because popular things don't always last, they might just be a fad. **When picking a career think both short and long term!**
What does your **Theme** look like?

What Is "Success"

What do you think it means to be successful? Why?	

Your Community

What is something your community does together?	

Your Economy

How is your families spending impacted by the economy?	

What is "Normal"

Who do you look to help you know what is "normal?"	

Your Entertainment

Gives some examples of apps, shows or music that you like:	

Understanding your identity is key to being confident when making choices. **Who are you and who do you want to be!**
2
Now Showing:
Staring
GO! Rosco!
DT-7C
It helps to reflect on your **background**, **plot** and **theme**!
Okay we need to get back to watering plants!

Step 2:
Study identity and identify how you see it guiding your life.

Beep-Beep-Beeeep!

Share something from each of these categories that have shaped your identity:

Background (BIRTH)	Plot (CHOOSE)	Theme (SCENE)
How did this set you up in life?	How has this changed your life?	Has this been a + or - influence in your life?

How do I?

This is a question that will help us better understand ourselves. **When we understand our personality it helps us be more efficient, meaning getting more done with less effort.**

Personality:(How):
Personality is the way you think, feel, and act. It's what makes you unique and influences how you respond to the world.

Key Word

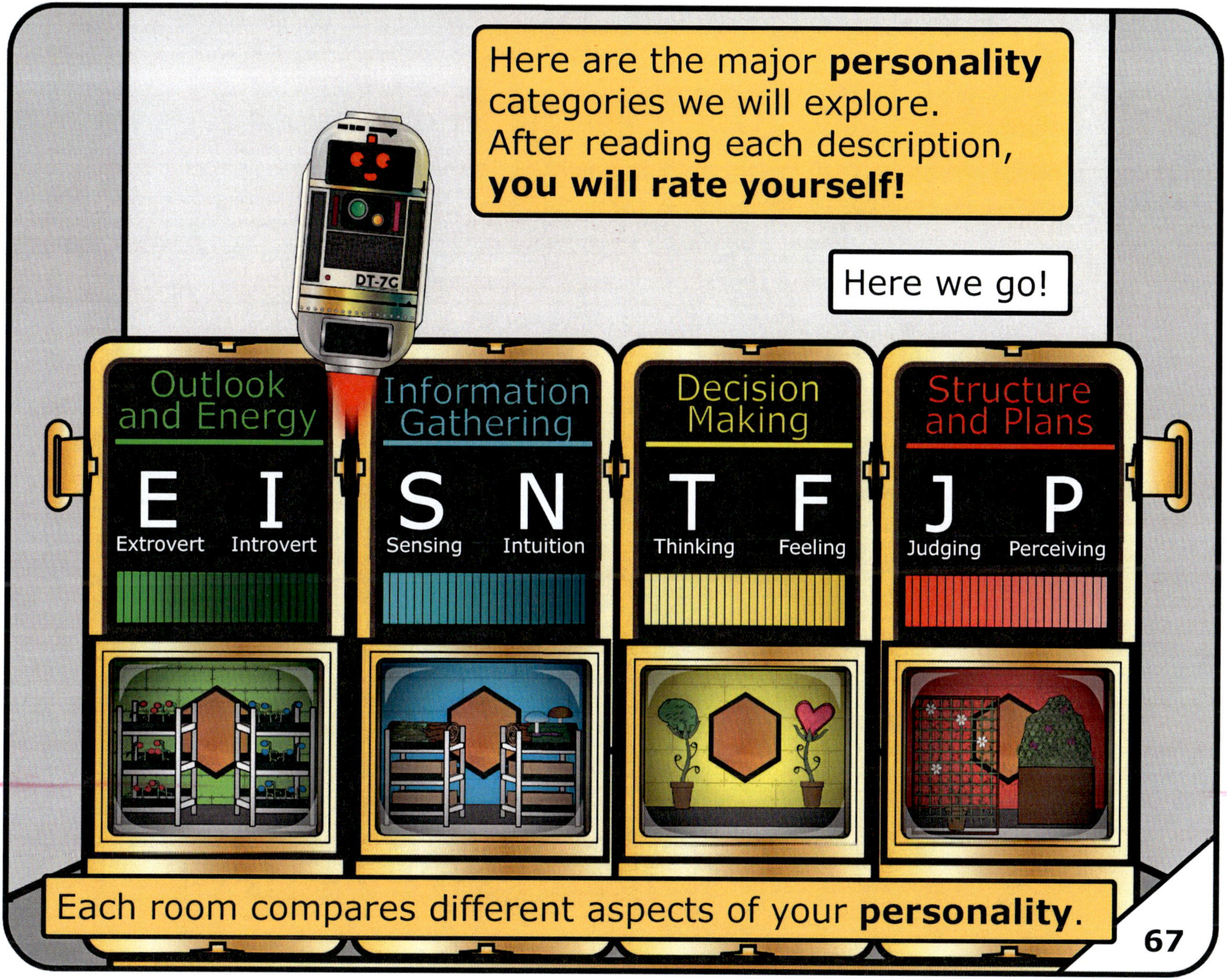
Here are the major **personality** categories we will explore. After reading each description, **you will rate yourself!**
Here we go!
DT-7G
Outlook and Energy
E Extrovert
I Introvert
Information Gathering
S Sensing
N Intuition
Decision Making
T Thinking
F Feeling
Structure and Plans
J Judging
P Perceiving
Each room compares different aspects of your **personality**.

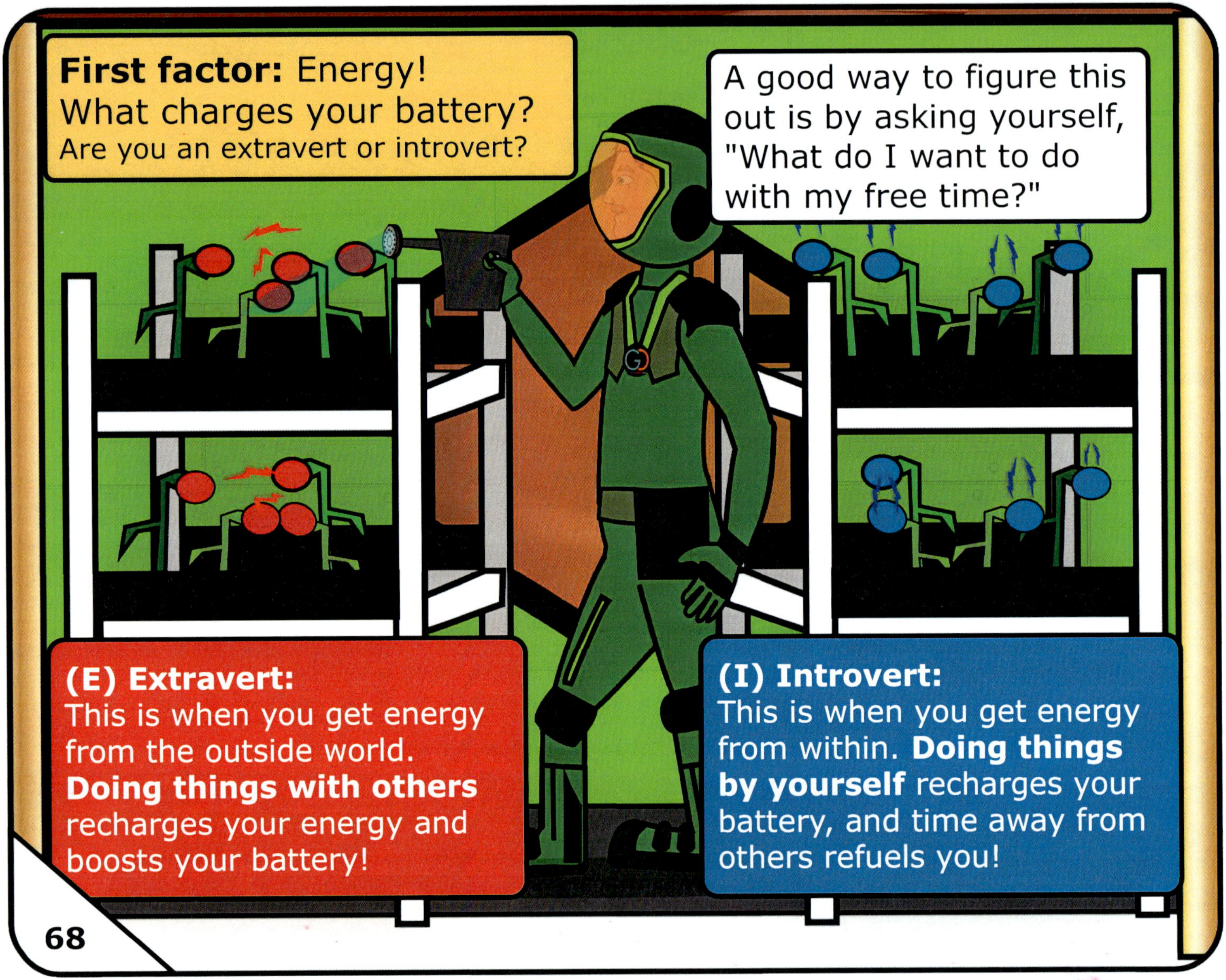
First factor: Energy!
What charges your battery?
Are you an extravert or introvert?
A good way to figure this out is by asking yourself, "What do I want to do with my free time?"
(E) Extravert:
This is when you get energy from the outside world. Doing things with others recharges your energy and boosts your battery!
(I) Introvert:
This is when you get energy from within. Doing things by yourself recharges your battery, and time away from others refuels you!

What are some jobs that would fit people with these personalities?

(E) Extravert:

For example:
A person who gets energy from others might like being a server. You're always meeting new people!

(I) Introvert:

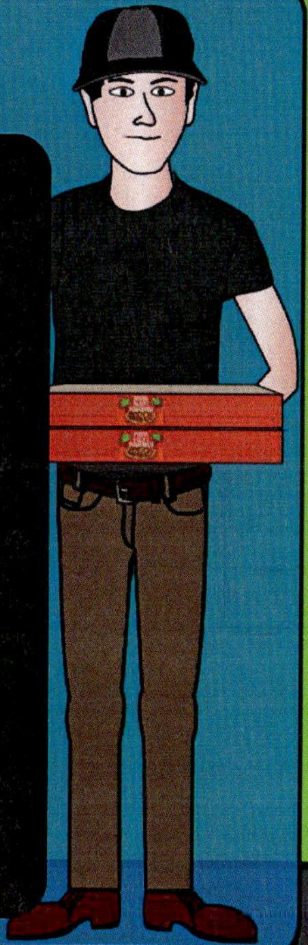

For Example:
A person who gets energy from time alone might like being a food delivery driver. They spend a lot of time alone while traveling.

Regardless of your personality type, any job will require you to work with people at times. **Do your best to be respectful and helpful!**

Which of these phrases do you most identify with?
Check off what describes you best!

(E) Extravert:

	I love working in groups, I get better ideas when we talk them out.
	I look forward to hanging out with friends after school.
	I feel recharged when I go to events or activities.
	I often speak up first in class discussions.
	I like being where the action is, celebrations, games, or clubs.
	I get excited to meet new people.
	I enjoy helping others face-to-face.
	I'm more productive when I'm around people.

(I) Introvert:

	I feel calm when I have quiet time to think.
	I like reading, drawing, or playing games by myself.
	I recharge by spending time in my room or going for walks.
	I prefer texting over phone calls.
	I take time to think before I speak.
	I enjoy solo projects where I can work at my own pace.
	I like hanging out with one or two close friends.
	I do my best thinking when it's quiet.

Energy

Score yourself by filling in the box that best describes you!

E **Extrovert** — **Introvert** **I**

You get energy from interacting with others.

You get energy from time by yourself.

What does this means for you:

Second factor: Information!
How do you like to get information?

"What do I need to feel in the know?"

(S) Sensing:
This is when you trust your hands-on experience to understand the world. **I am more detail oriented; I like facts and details.** You want to know the facts and be able to test them.

(N) Intuition:
This is when you trust ideas, patterns, and thinking to understand the world.
I focus more on the big picture; I like patterns and possibilities. You trust your thinking; you don't have to know for sure.

What are some jobs that would fit people with these personalities?

(S) Sensing:

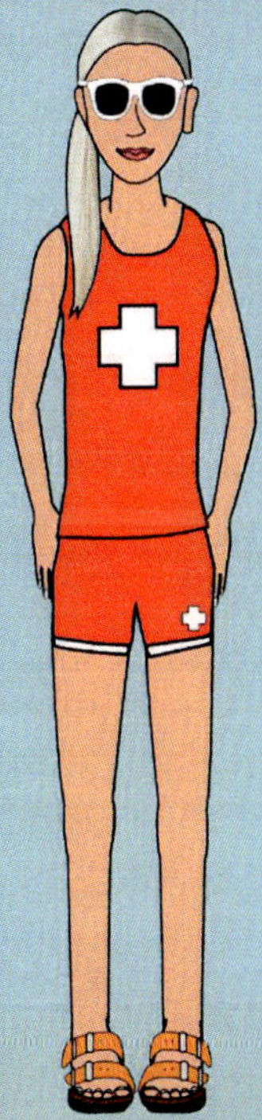

For Example:
A person who is more observant might like being a lifeguard. They need to be aware of what is happening around them.

(N) Intuition:

For Example:
A person who is more big-picture focused might like being a para. They help students understand different ideas.

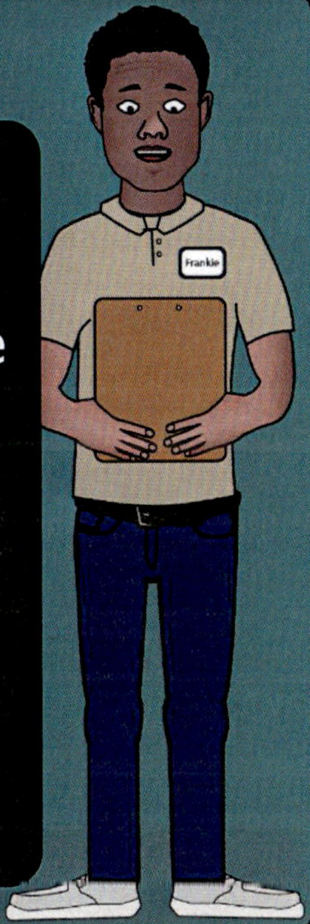

Working together we can accomplish all the little and big things!

Which of these phrases do you most identify with?
Check off what describes you best!

(S) Sensing:		(N) Intuition:	
	I remember details like dates, names, and directions.		I like imagining how things could be better.
	I like hands-on activities like cooking, building, or drawing.		I ask a lot of "What if...?" questions.
	I want clear steps before starting a task.		I don't need every detail to get started.
	I prefer real-life examples over just theories.		I like making connections between big ideas.
	I notice when something's out of place.		I enjoy solving creative problems.
	I trust what I've experienced before.		I sometimes miss little things because I'm thinking ahead.
	I do well with routines and instructions.		I love coming up with new possibilities or inventions.
	I focus on what's happening right now.		I prefer trying new things over repeating the same steps.

Information

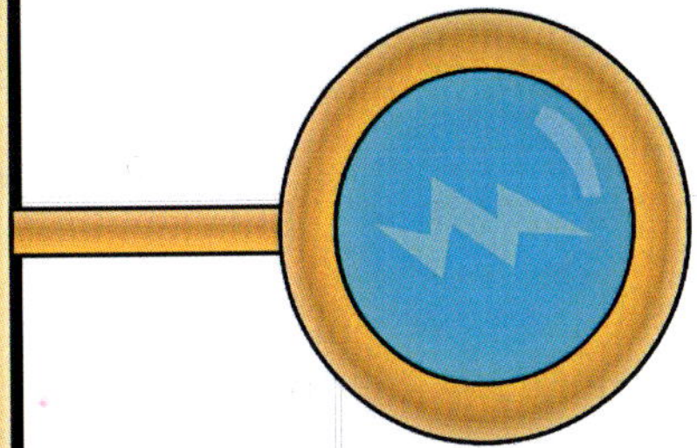

Score yourself by filling in the box that best describes you!

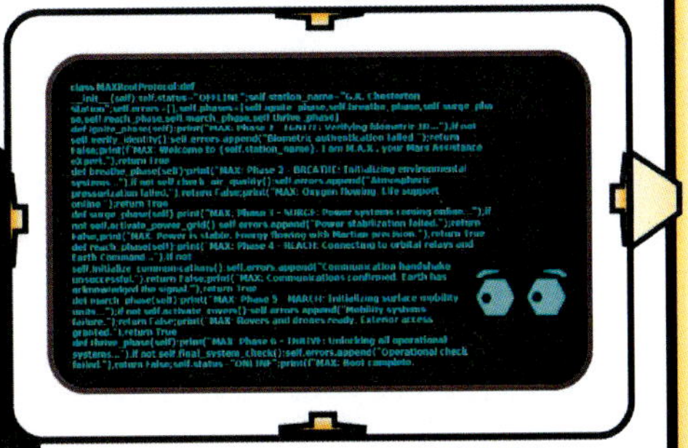

S **Sensing** | **Intuition** **N**

You want to know the little details. ⟷ You want to know the big idea.

What does this means for you:

Third factor: Decisions!
What drives your choices?

Do more of your sentences start with I think or I feel?

(T) Thinking:

You rely on your brain when making decisions.
You use reason and logic to decide.
To you a person should think things through before deciding!

(F) Feeling:

You rely on your heart when making decisions.
You follow your feelings and values to guide your choices.
To you a person should decide by trusting their heart!

What are some jobs that would fit people with these personalities?

(T) Thinking:

For Example:
A thinker might enjoy working as a mechanic. You find the parts to fix the vehicle, it's like solving a puzzle. Cars don't care how you feel.

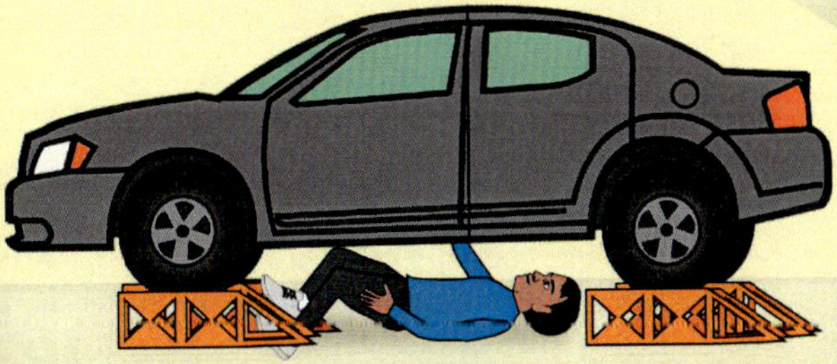

(F) Feeling:

For Example:
A feeler might enjoy working as a nurse. You help people recover and pay attention to how they are feeling. Recovery requires emotional connection.

Extremes can get us in trouble, always try to have a balance of both!

Which of these phrases do you most identify with?
Check off what describes you best!

(T) Thinking:

	I try to stay calm and solve problems step by step.
	I ask, "Does this make sense?" before deciding.
	I value fairness and facts.
	I focus on getting things done correctly.
	I don't let emotions get in the way of a good decision.
	I enjoy puzzles, strategy games, or math problems.
	I might come off as blunt, but I'm just being honest.
	I like fixing things that are broken.

(F) Feeling:

	I ask, "How will this affect others?" before deciding.
	I care about people's feelings and try to include everyone.
	I enjoy helping people feel better.
	I'm good at sensing how others feel.
	I try to avoid conflict and keep peace.
	I like doing kind things just because.
	I feel happiest when I'm making a difference.
	I make decisions based on what feels right.

Decisions

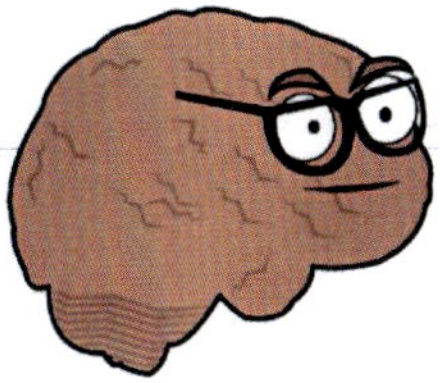

Score yourself by filling in the box that best describes you!

T **Thinking** ←→ **Feeling** **F**

You make choices through your reasons.

You make choices through your emotions.

What does this means for you:

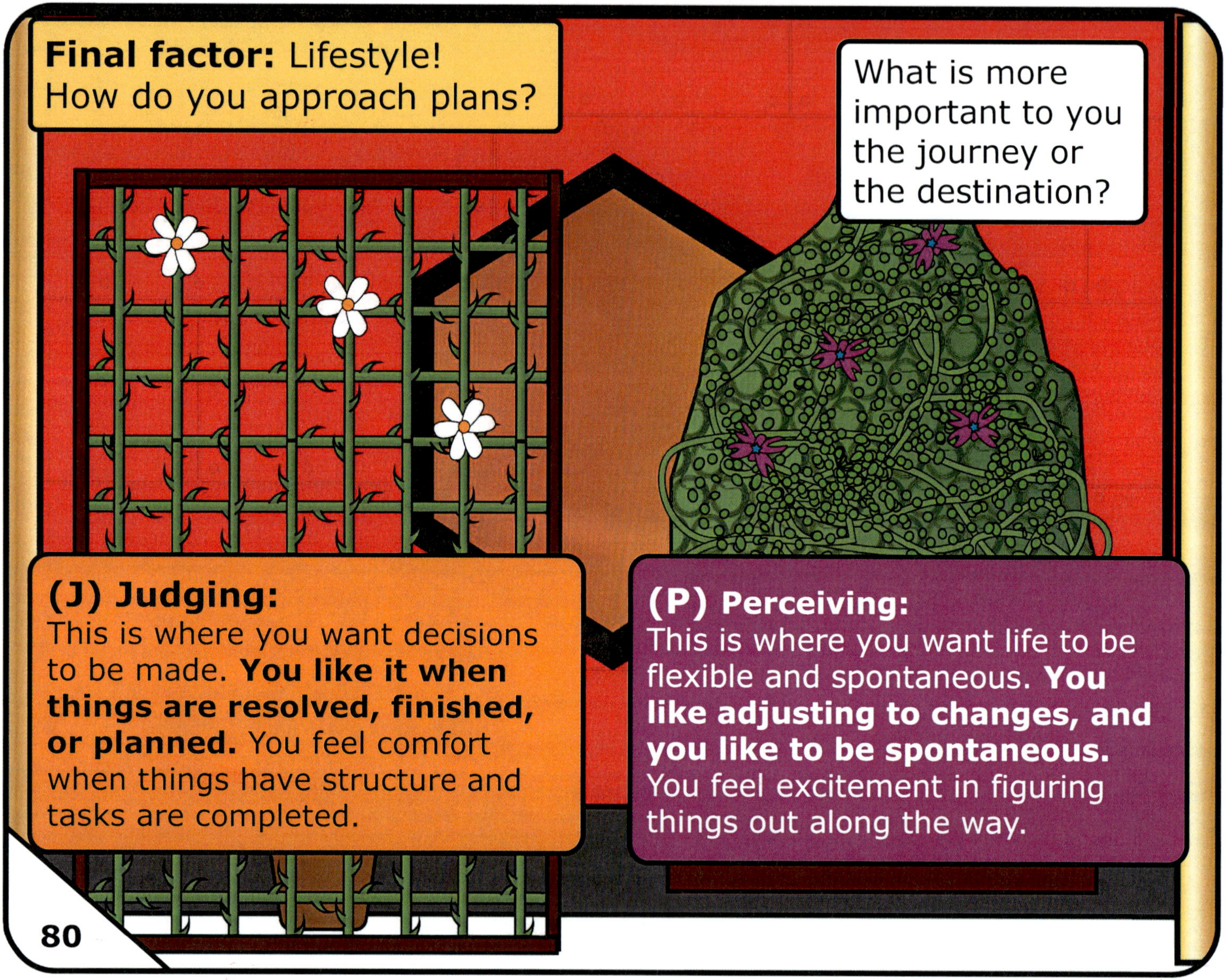
Final factor: Lifestyle!
How do you approach plans?
What is more important to you the journey or the destination?
(J) Judging:
This is where you want decisions to be made. **You like it when things are resolved, finished, or planned.** You feel comfort when things have structure and tasks are completed.
(P) Perceiving:
This is where you want life to be flexible and spontaneous. **You like adjusting to changes, and you like to be spontaneous.** You feel excitement in figuring things out along the way.

What are some jobs that would fit people with these personalities?

(J) Judging:

For Example:
A person who likes things organized might enjoy being a receptionist. They help people get things done.

(P) Perceiving:

For Example:
A person who likes open, adventurous work might enjoy being a dog walker. You never know what's going to happen.

If you need help accomplishing things, make a checklist.
If you need help being flexible, give yourself permission to relax.

Which of these phrases do you most identify with?
Check off what describes you best!

(J) Judging:		(P) Perceiving	
	I feel good when I check things off my to-do list.		I like seeing where the day takes me.
	I like knowing what the schedule is ahead of time.		I don't mind changing plans last minute.
	I plan my day so I'm not rushed.		I'm creative and think of new ways to do things.
	I prefer clear rules and expectations.		I work best under pressure or near deadlines.
	I don't like last-minute changes.		I like options, not strict rules.
	I often finish homework early.		I jump between projects based on what excites me.
	I set goals and stick to them.		I'm good at adjusting when things go wrong.
	I clean my room or organize things without being asked.		I bring energy and fun into new situations.

Lifestyle

Score yourself by filling in the box that best describes you!

J Judging ⟵ ⟶ Perceiving **P**

You like having things figured out.

You like when things are open and free.

What does this means for you:

How does this connect to earning?
Knowing your personality will help you find a job that fits you! It will also help you to better under the other people you work with!

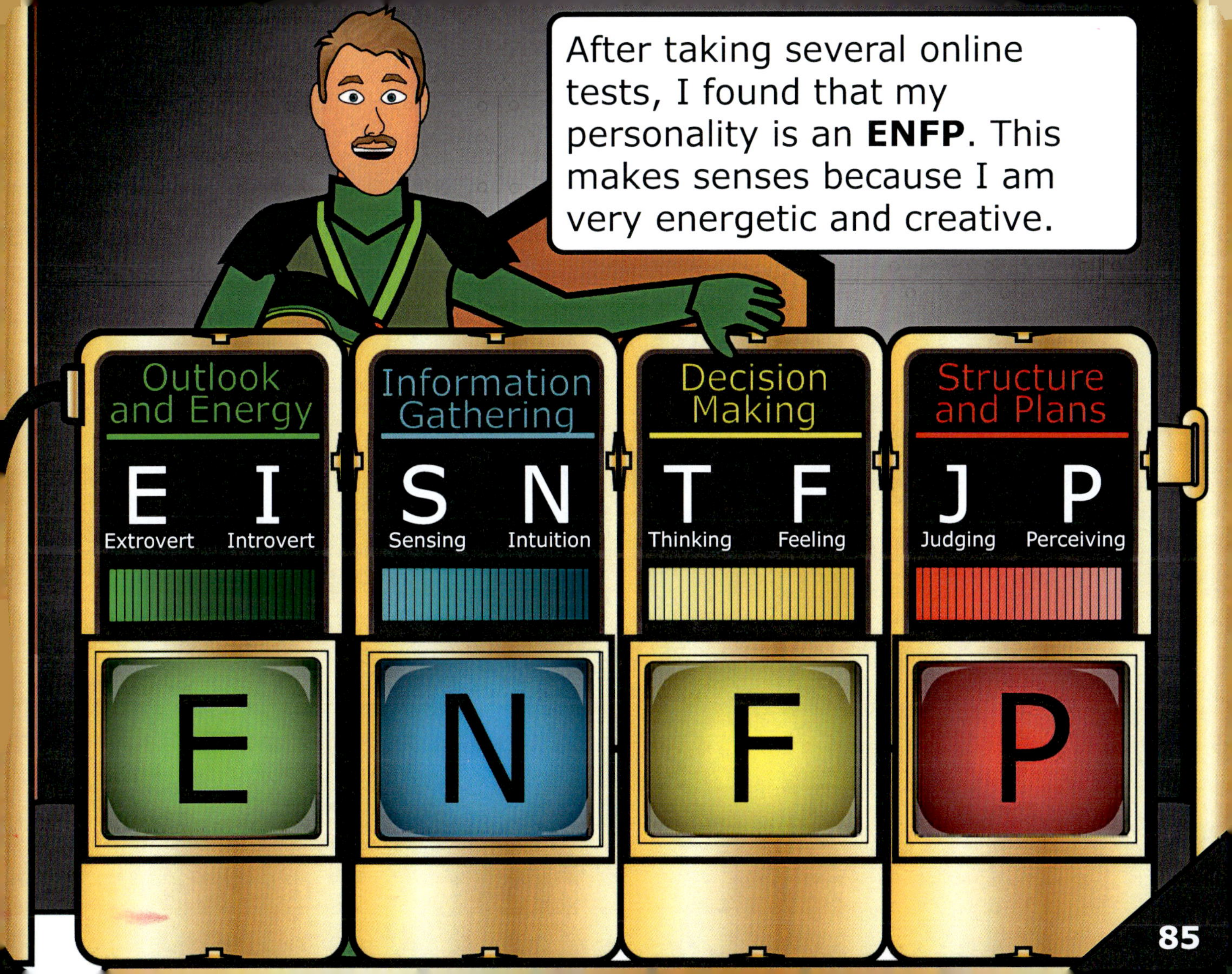

After taking several online tests, I found that my personality is an **ENFP**. This makes senses because I am very energetic and creative.
Outlook and Energy
E Extrovert
I Introvert
Information Gathering
S Sensing
N Intuition
Decision Making
T Thinking
F Feeling
Structure and Plans
J Judging
P Perceiving
E N F P

Now it is your turn! You can use your scores from the rooms or to determine your personality type or your can take a **free Myers Briggs online personality test**.

See if you can find any friends who share your personality!

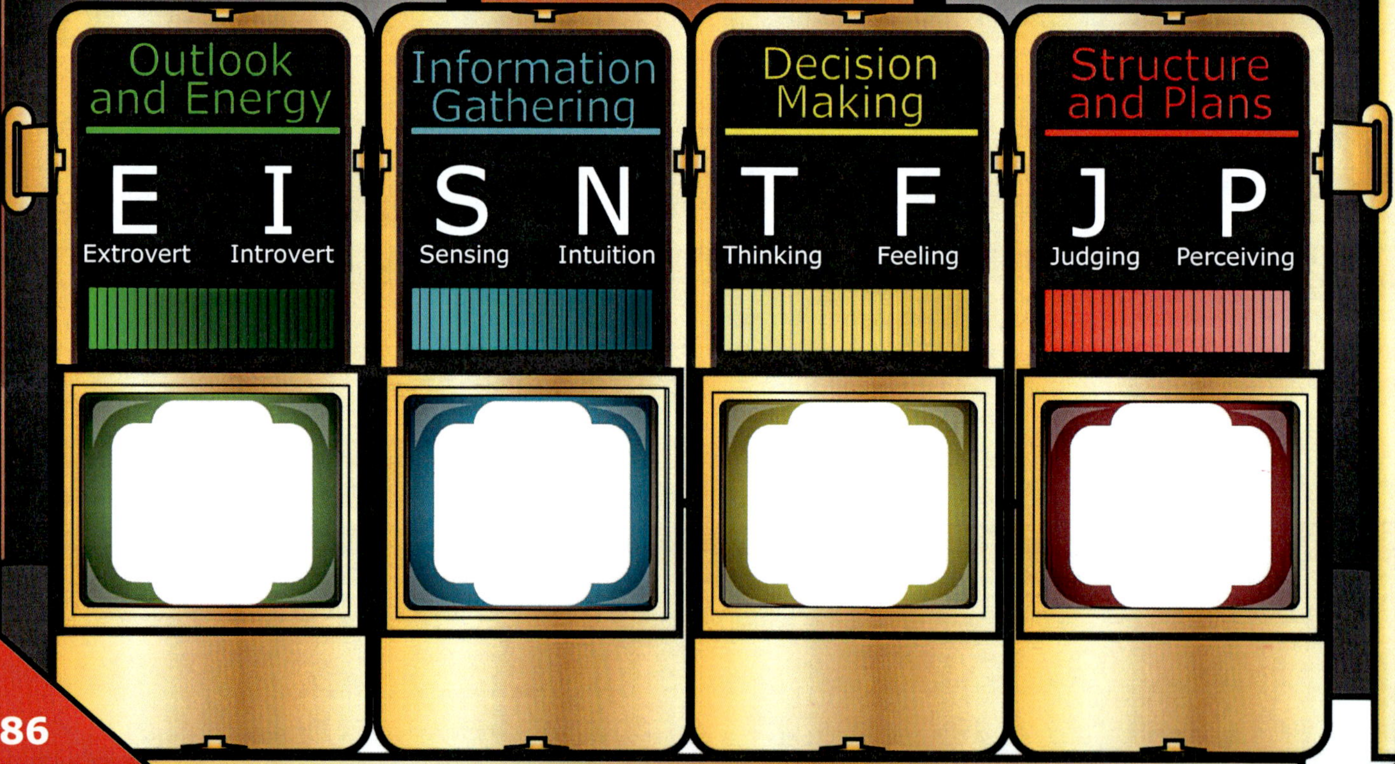

Step 3: Recognize your personality and how it shapes your choices.

Beep-Beep!

How does your personality shape how you work? Give several examples!

Who is someone with a personality like yours? What do you like about how they do things?

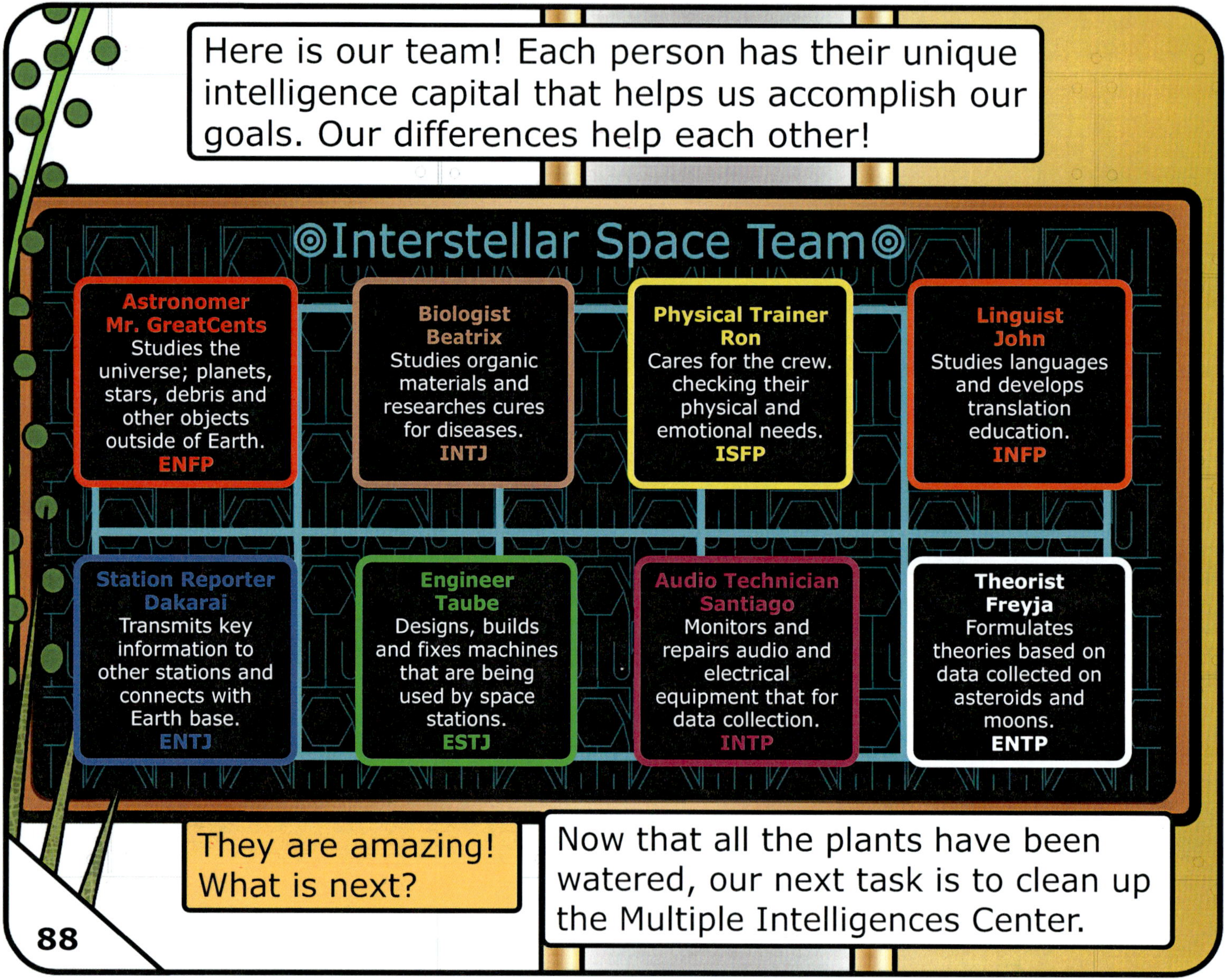
Here is our team! Each person has their unique intelligence capital that helps us accomplish our goals. Our differences help each other!
Interstellar Space Team
Astronomer Mr. GreatCents Studies the universe; planets, stars, debris and other objects outside of Earth. ENFP
Biologist Beatrix Studies organic materials and researches cures for diseases. INTJ
Physical Trainer Ron Cares for the crew. checking their physical and emotional needs. ISFP
Linguist John Studies languages and develops translation education. INFP
Station Reporter Dakarai Transmits key information to other stations and connects with Earth base. ENTJ
Engineer Taube Designs, builds and fixes machines that are being used by space stations. ESTJ
Audio Technician Santiago Monitors and repairs audio and electrical equipment that for data collection. INTP
Theorist Freyja Formulates theories based on data collected on asteroids and moons. ENTP
They are amazing! What is next?
Now that all the plants have been watered, our next task is to clean up the Multiple Intelligences Center.

To understand careers, you need to have a basic understanding of **economics!**

Economics:
The study of how people use money and resources to get what they need and want.

Key Word

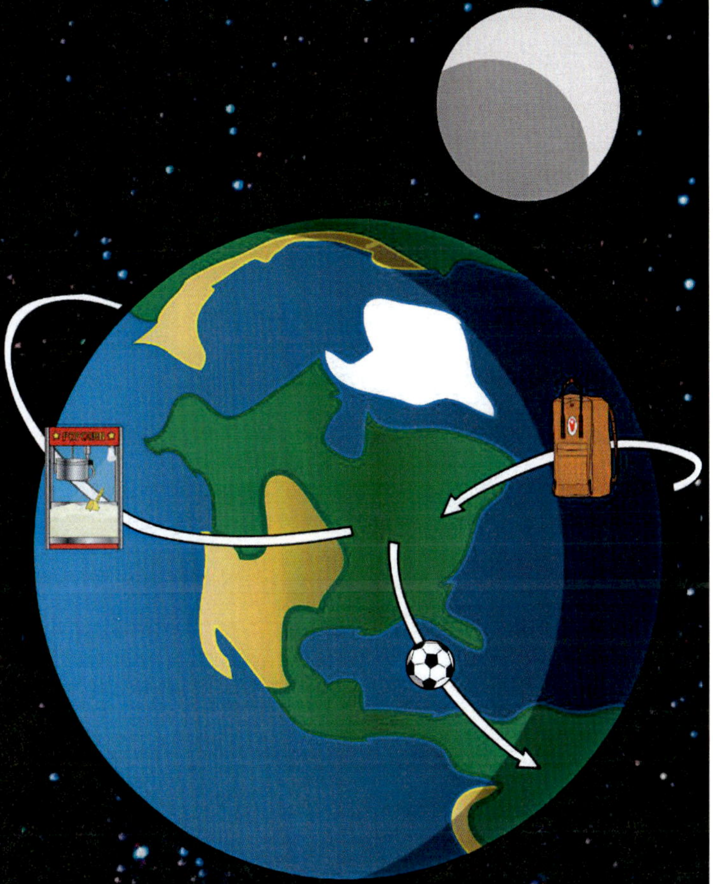

You have wants and needs. Without something to eat you would starve! However, instead of finding your food **you can buy it**. You give a business money and they give you food. With the money you paid **they pay their employees**, buy new supply and grow. We are all connected and need each other!

Producers:
The people who make goods and provide services.

People are a part of a cycle of working and spending!

Consumers:
The people who buy and use goods and services.

Goods:
Things you can buy and own.
Examples: phones, food, clothes, etc.

Wants:
Things you would like but could live without.
Examples: games, candy, perfume, etc.

Services:
Actions or activities that someone does for you for a fee.
Examples: haircuts, bowling, streaming services, mowing the lawn, etc.

Needs:
Things you must have to stay alive and stay safe.
Examples: food, clothes, water, and shelter.

As a producer you: Get paid!

As a consumer you: Pay to get!

Producers

Think of the word "product." When working a job you are helping others through what you do!

Business Owner

Goods they can sell:
1.
2.
3.
4.
5.

Nurse

What services does a nurse provide?
X

Consumers

Think of the word "customer." When you buy things you are helping people earn money!

You!

What are some things you need?
1.
2.
3.
4.

What are some things you want?
1.
2.
3.
4.

Santiago is in charge of making sure all the audio equipment. Without him we wouldn't be able to work and receive our funds for our research. Through earning this money we get paid.

Beatrix is in charge of food production. She helps set up growing stations that provide much of the food used at our bases. Without something to eat our staff wouldn't be able to accomplish much!
Nutrition Facts
4 servings per container
Serving Size
Amount per serving
Calories 170
% Daily Value*
Total Fat 1.5g 2%
Saturated Fat 0g 0%
Trans Fat 0g
Cholesterol 0mg 0%
Sodium 0mg 0%
Total Carbohydrate 36g 13%
Dietary Fiber 0g 14%
Total Sugars 5g
Included 0g Added Sugars 0%
Protein 5g
Vitamin D 0mcg 0%
Calcium 4mg 0%
Iron 1mg 6%
Potassium 330mg 8%
*The % Daily Value tells you how much a nutrient in a serving of food contributes to a daily diet. 2000 calories a day is used for general nutrition advice.
Calories per gram:
Fat 9 Carbohydate 4 Protein 4

This is why it is so important to build your **human capital**, understand your **identity** and your **personality**.
This building meets all requirements for space based safety.
With my **unique skills** I am able to bring in **income** that will help us continue to grow our team's mission.
Beep-Beep!
Yeah, it is still very windy out there!

Different goods and services require different amounts of human capital.
Could you give some examples?
Sure! Think of a fast food worker and an aerospace engineer. A teen could learn how to work at a restaurant in a day, whereas it takes years for a person to learn how to build rockets.
Still in High School
This certifies that
Tim Kell
10th grade
High School
GC University
GreatCents
Our Town, Nebraska
GC University
GreatCents
Our Town, Nebraska
GreatCents University
Taube Lovejoy
PHD in Aerospace Engineering

Generally in an economy people with **unique skills** and **intelligence** will be paid more for their talents! Check it out!

The phrase, **"Learning is earning,"** really holds some truth! It's not guaranteed, but it's often true.

Time to clean up the Intelligence Center. This room is dedicated to explore the different ways that people are smart.

For a long time people believed being smart really just meant you could score well on a test. This view was very limited.

Yes! The ability to communicate with others is an intelligence just like you would solve a math problem. The Multiple Intelligences helps give us a more full view of intelligence!

The Multiple Intelligences:

This is the theory that there are multiple types of intelligence that a person can learn. Generally, jobs and careers will utilize these strengths and develop areas of weakness.

Gardner, Howard. Frames of Mind: The Theory of Multiple Intelligences. Basic Books, 1983.

Key Word

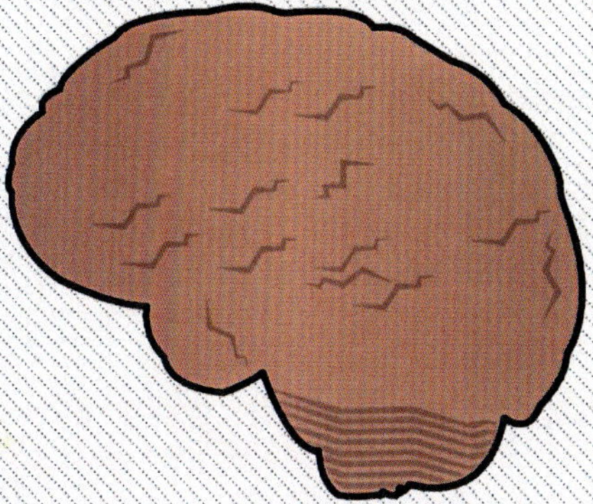

How do we know they exist?

Brain Locations

- Different parts of our brain are connected with certain intelligences.

Shared Skills

- All over the world people exercise these types of intelligences.

Ability to Learn and Master

- You are able to be taught how to do skills related to the intelligence and even master it through practice.

We each have different types of **"smart"**.

Your **thoughts**, **feelings** and **behaviors** are connected and so are your types of **intelligence**.

Academic

These intelligences required learning information and using that knowledge.

Builder

These intelligences require training and practice. It's not just know, but doing!

Character

These intelligences are built on relationships with others and yourself.

Next, we look at each of **the different types of intelligence**, consider which is your strongest and weakest. Just like with our **identity** and **personality** we are always growing.
What should they expect to see?
I will show you an example!

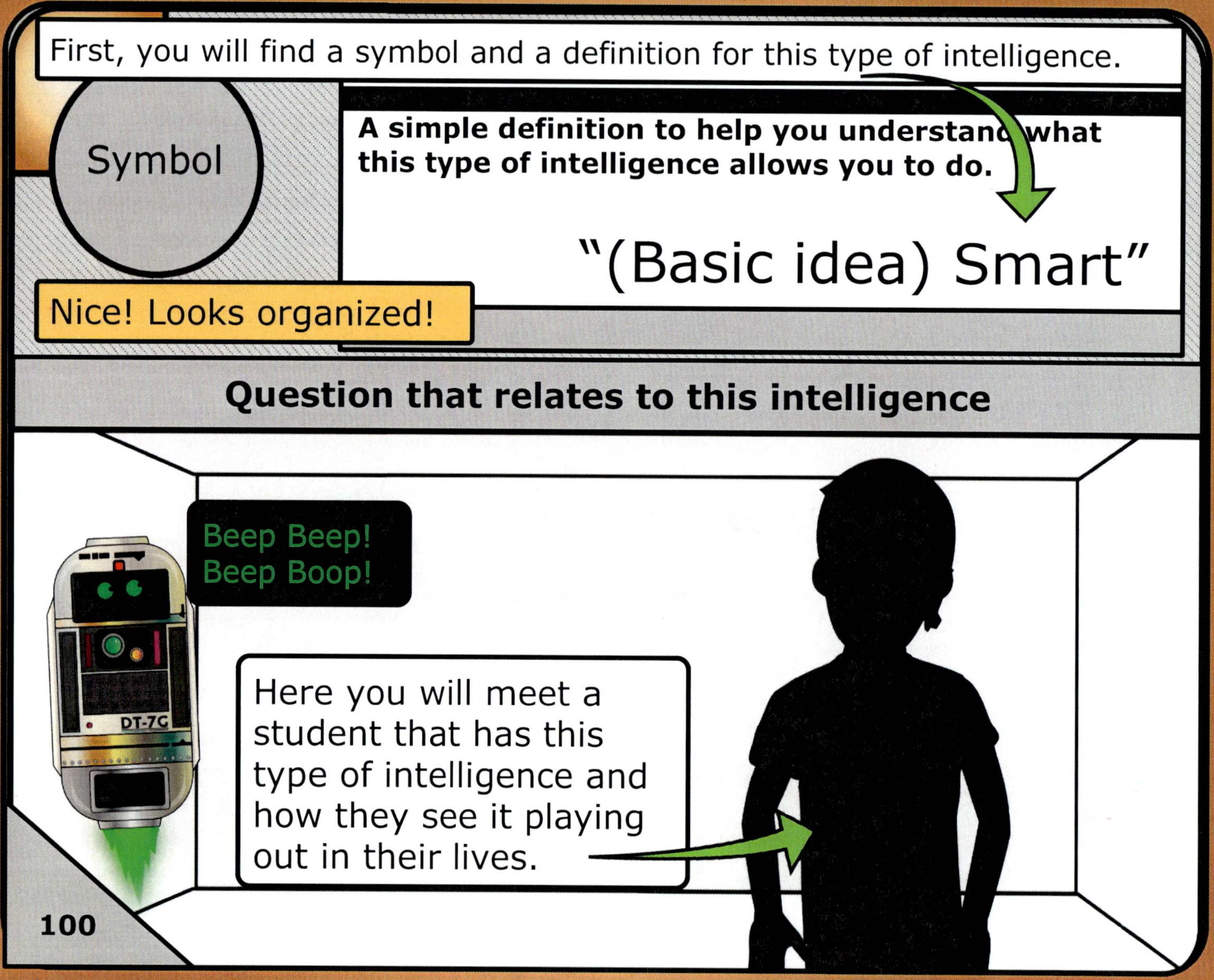
First, you will find a symbol and a definition for this type of intelligence.
Symbol
A simple definition to help you understand what this type of intelligence allows you to do.
"(Basic idea) Smart"
Nice! Looks organized!
Question that relates to this intelligence
Beep Beep!
Beep Boop!
DT-7G
Here you will meet a student that has this type of intelligence and how they see it playing out in their lives.

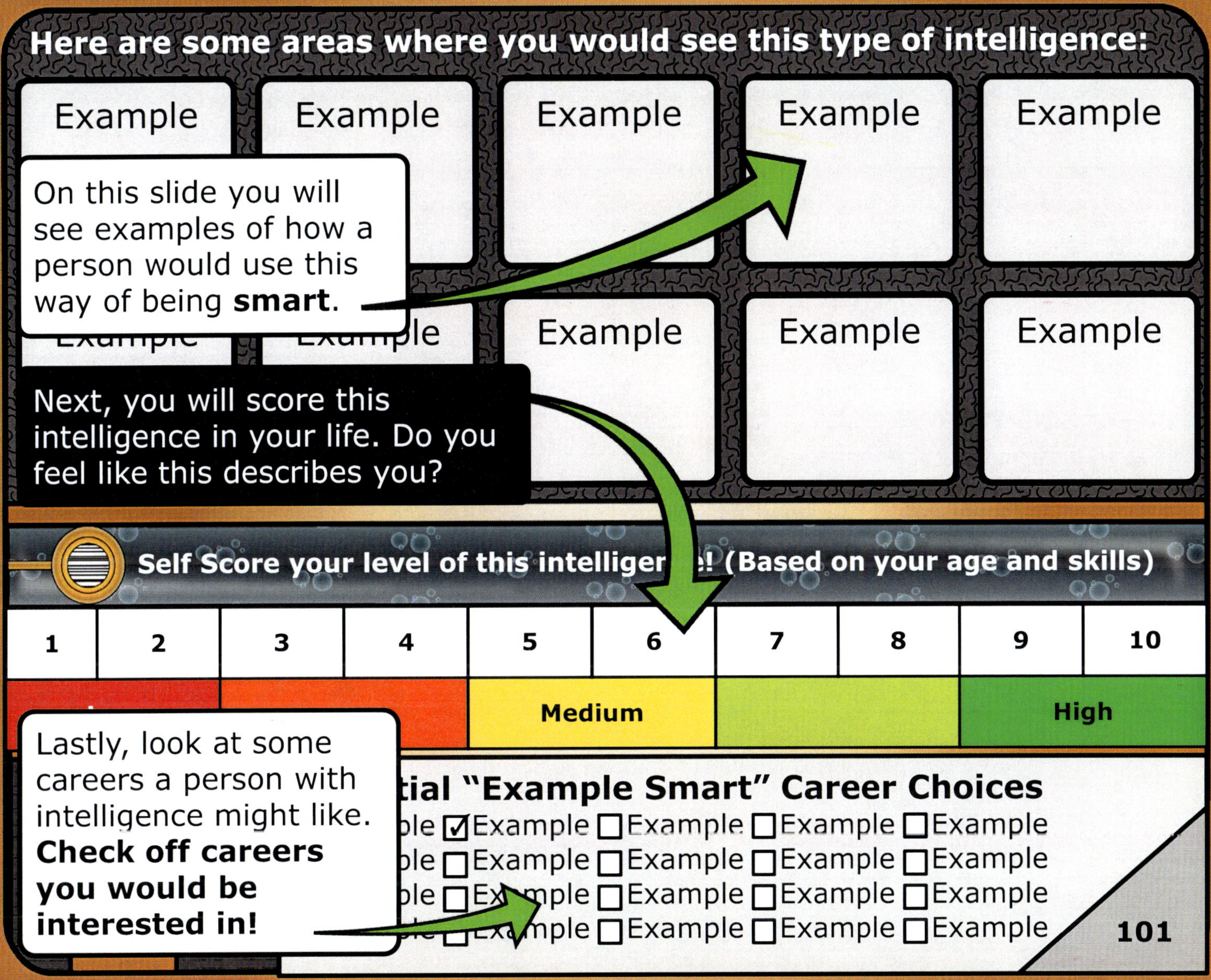

Here are some areas where you would see this type of intelligence:
Example
Example
Example
Example
Example
Example
Example
Example
On this slide you will see examples of how a person would use this way of being **smart**.
Next, you will score this intelligence in your life. Do you feel like this describes you?
Self Score your level of this intellige e! (Based on your age and skills)
1 2 3 4 5 6 7 8 9 10
Medium
High
Lastly, look at some careers a person with intelligence might like. **Check off careers you would be interested in!**
tial "Example Smart" Career Choices
☑ Example ☐ Example ☐ Example ☐ Example
☐ Example ☐ Example ☐ Example ☐ Example
☐ Example ☐ Example ☐ Example ☐ Example
☐ Example ☐ Example ☐ Example ☐ Example
101

Your Mathematical Intelligence:

This is the ability to understand and solve logical and mathematical problems. It means being able to work with numbers, shapes, and patterns to find solutions.

"Math Smart"

Can you do Addition? Subtraction? Multiplication? Division?

Hi! My name is **Zora**, and I'm in 8th grade. Out of all the intelligences, I think "**Math Smart**" is my strongest. I really enjoy anything that involves problem-solving.

Every Saturday, my family has game night, and we love playing board games. **Strategy** really gets my mind working, I can think through all the steps!

My favorite class in school is **Math**. I joined Science Olympiad this year to build an egg car.

My team and I came up with an awesome design, and I'm really hoping we can win! I would love to be an **engineer** someday!

Here are some areas where you would see this type of intelligence:

Basic Math + - x ÷	Algebra 4x+2=12	Geometry	Statistics	Working $ with $ Money
Puzzles	Board games	Science Experiments	Designing and Building	Problem Solving (Investigating)

Score your level of this intelligence! (Based on your age and skills)

1	2	3	4	5	6	7	8	9	10
Low				Medium				High	

"Math Smart" Example Careers Checklist

☐ Accountant ☐ Architect ☐ Astronomer ☐ Banker ☐ Detective
☐ Doctor ☐ Economist ☐ Engineer ☐ Financial Planner
☐ Lawyer ☐ Math Teacher ☐ Manager ☐ Programmer
☐ Scientist ☐ Statistician ☐ Video Game Developer

Your Linguistic Intelligence:

This is the ability to understand and interpret words, then use them to express ideas clearly. It's about listening, reading, and creating sentences that make sense to others.

"Word Smart"

Can you Read? Write? Speak? Listen?

Hey! I'm **Iris**, and I'm in 7th grade.
I'm very **"Word Smart"** and love anything that involves stories, whether it's reading, writing, speaking, or even listening sometimes.

I'm the youngest of four sisters, and, as you can imagine, it was hard to get attention! I like to be the comedian of the family, and sometimes I write funny stories to **share** with my friends. I went to camp this past summer, and I was known as the storyteller!

At school, I find that I enjoy **Language Arts class** the most. The flow of sentence structure just makes sense to me. I want to do something with stories when I grow up, a **writer** or **director**!

Here are some areas where you would see this type of intelligence:

- Reading
- Writing
- Business Sales $
- Grammar: is vs are
- Speech
- Languages 語言
- Rules: You should "..."
- Movies
- Event Planning
- Spelling

Score your level of this intelligence! (Based on your age and skills)

1	2	3	4	5	6	7	8	9	10
Low				Medium				High	

"Word Smart" Example Careers Checklist

☐ Actor ☐ Author ☐ Copywriter ☐ Editor ☐ English Teacher
☐ Fundraiser ☐ Journalist ☐ Librarian ☐ News Reporter
☐ Paralegal ☐ Podcaster ☐ Salesperson ☐ Secretary
☐ Social Media Manager ☐ Translator ☐ Tourism

Your Naturalistic Intelligence:

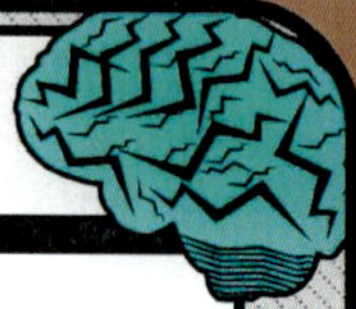

This is the ability to recognize and understand processes in the natural world. It involves noticing nature's details or using the scientific method to explore how things work.

"Nature Smart"

Can you identify a Animal? Bird? Fish? Plant? Flowers?

Hello! I'm **Jude**, and this is **Rover**. We have a blue jay in sight! My grandpa says I'm pretty **"Nature Smart."** Learning about animals, birds, plants, trees—really, everything in nature—fills me with wonder. Life is so cool!

I live on a farm with my grandparents. Even though I'm in a wheelchair, I still help with gardening and **taking care of the animals**. I also enjoy hunting with Grandpa. Camping is another passion of mine; I love being outdoors!

I'm in 9th grade, and **Science class** is my favorite—especially biology. I'd like a job someday where I can do **experiments** and make discoveries.

Here are some areas where you would see this type of intelligence:

- Scientific Method
  - ?Question?
  - -Hypothesis-
  - -Experiment-
  - !Conclusion!
- Observing Animals
- Identifying Bugs
- Collecting Plant seeds
- Protecting Forests
- Studying the Elements (11 Na Sodium)
- Gardening
- Caring for Parks
- Recording Nature
- Caring for Pets

Score your level of this intelligence! (Based on your age and skills)

1	2	3	4	5	6	7	8	9	10
Low				Medium				High	

"Nature Smart" Example Career Checklist

☐ Animal Trainer ☐ Arborist ☐ Archeologist ☐ Botanist
☐ Breeder ☐ Farmer ☐ Gardener ☐ Geologist ☐ Landscaping
☐ Biologist ☐ Meteorologist ☐ Park Ranger ☐ Teacher
☐ Scientist ☐ Veterinarian ☐ Photographer ☐ Zoologist

Math Smart

How do people use math outside of school?

What helps you stay calm when solving problems? Give an example!

Word Smart

Who do you think is a great writer, speaker or actor?

How could strong communication help in life?

Nature Smart

How can people take care of the environment?

How do you help care for living things?

Academic

These intelligences help you learn, think, and understand information. Without them, you wouldn't be able to problem-solve, read, write, or understand the laws of nature.

Your Bodily Kinesthetic intelligence:

This is the ability to understand and control your body's movements and abilities. It shows up in physical activities like sports, training, and coordination.

"Body Smart"

Can you Stand? Sit? Walk? Jump? Climb? Crawl?

Hey, I'm **Pablo**! I just got into middle school, and I'm so excited to compete in sports! I'm actually part of a local traveling team. My older brother says I'm **"body smart."** We like to work out together. Practicing sports makes me feel alive!

My parents are very intentional about helping us learn new skills. Dad has taught my brother and me how to do a lot of home construction. He wants us to know **how to work with our hands**. Last week, we put up walls in the basement. Someday, I'd like to have my own set of power tools.

Physical education (PE) is my favorite class at school. I'm always up for trying new sports!
I want to be a **firefighter** when I grow up.

Here are some areas where you would see this type of intelligence:

- Exercise
- Lifting
- Sports Activities
- Acting
- Balance
- Dancing
- Working with your hands
- Swimming
- Muscle Memory **Practice!**
- Typing

Score your level of this intelligence! (Based on your age and skills)

1	2	3	4	5	6	7	8	9	10
Low				Medium				High	

"Body Smart" Example Careers Checklist

- ☐ Athlete
- ☐ Carpenter
- ☐ Coach
- ☐ Construction
- ☐ Criminal Justice
- ☐ Dancer
- ☐ Farmer
- ☐ Mover
- ☐ Jeweler
- ☐ Magician
- ☐ Massage therapist
- ☐ Mechanic
- ☐ Military
- ☐ Personal Trainer
- ☐ PE Teacher
- ☐ Physical Therapist

Your Musical Intelligence:

This is the ability to hear and recognize different parts of music and to reproduce those sounds with your voice or an instrument.

"Music Smart"

Can you Sing? Listen to Music? Write a Song?

Hey, come on in! I'm **Frankie**. This is my Uncle Ryan's music store. He's in a band and away on a trip, so I'm filling in while he's gone. I've learned to play a handful of instruments, and my friends all say I'm **"Music Smart."**

Music is what drives me, **I'm always listening for a beat**. I just celebrated my 16th birthday, and my parents got me a drum set! I hope to be in a band like my uncle one day. He's also been teaching me how to work in a music studio. It's amazing how we can capture sound.

As you can imagine, I'm really involved at school with **Choir** and **Band**. I would like to help **produce music** for artist in the future!

Here are some areas where you would see this type of intelligence:

- Singing
- Playing Instruments
- Reading Sheet Music
- Recognizing Musical Keys (A, Cm)
- Writing Songs or Music
- Performing Music
- Listening to Music
- Concerts
- DJing
- Recording Music

Score your level of this intelligence! (Based on your age and skills)

1	2	3	4	5	6	7	8	9	10
Low				Medium				High	

"Music Smart" Example Careers Checklist

- ☐ Accompanist ☐ Artist Manager ☐ Audiologist ☐ Composer
- ☐ Conductor ☐ DJ ☐ Lyricist ☐ Music Arranger ☐ Publicist
- ☐ Music Teacher ☐ Musician ☐ Producer ☐ Engineer
- ☐ Singer ☐ Songwriter ☐ Vocal Coach

Your Spatial Intelligence:

This is the ability to visualize and understand dimensions, directions, and shapes. This intelligence uses imagination to create things in the real world.

"Picture Smart"

Can you draw a picture? Do you play games of watch TV?

Hey, I'm **Leona**, and I love painting! The ability to capture the world and put it on a canvas feels so creative! I've been working on a series of pictures that play with shapes, colors, and textures.

My dad is a doctor at the reservation. I like to tag along with him and paint flowers out in nature. My grandma lives there, and she taught me how to paint landscapes. She says I'm **"picture smart."** I'm really good at seeing different perspectives. I have a couple of paintings I want to enter in a contest.
This is my 7th-grade year, and as you can imagine, I really enjoy **art class**. I'm constantly doodling in all my other classes. I want to be a **painter**!

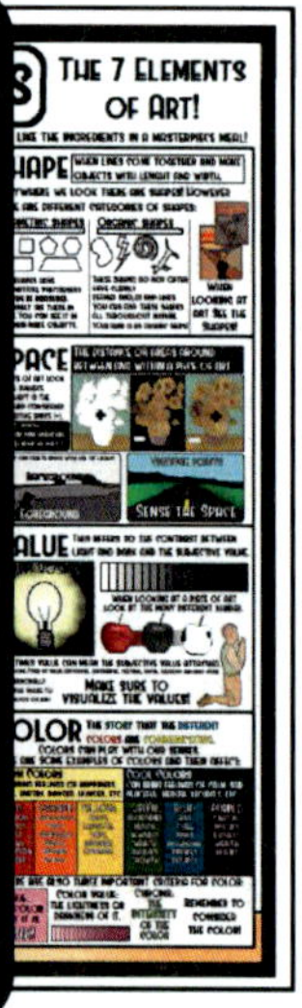

Here are some areas where you would see this type of intelligence:

Directions	Building	Graphic Design	Painting	Mazes
Hiking	Estimating Size	Predicting Movement	Maps	Organizing

Score your level of this intelligence! (Based on your age and skills)

1	2	3	4	5	6	7	8	9	10
Low				Medium				High	

"Picture Smart" Example Careers Checklist

- ■ Advertising ■ Animator ■ Architect ■ Artist ■ Cartographer
- ■ Construction ■ Fashion Designer ■ Graphic Designer
- ■ Illustrator ■ Interior Designer ■ Landscaping ■ Painter
- ■ Photographer ■ Physicist ■ Video ■ Web Design

Body Smart

What are some of your favorite physical activities?

How do movement and exercise affect your mood? Give an example!

Music Smart

What types of music do you enjoy most? Why?

Why is music important in cultures? Give examples!

Picture Smart

How do pictures help people understand information?

Are you good with directions? Ex. North, East, South & West. Explain.

Builder

These intelligences help you learn by doing, practicing, and creating. They are important for controlling your body, enjoying music, building skills, and organizing your world.

Your Intrapersonal Intelligence:

This is the ability to understand and analyze your own thoughts and emotions. It also helps you empathize with others because you can relate to their feelings.

"Self Smart"

Can you share one thing you like to do by yourself?

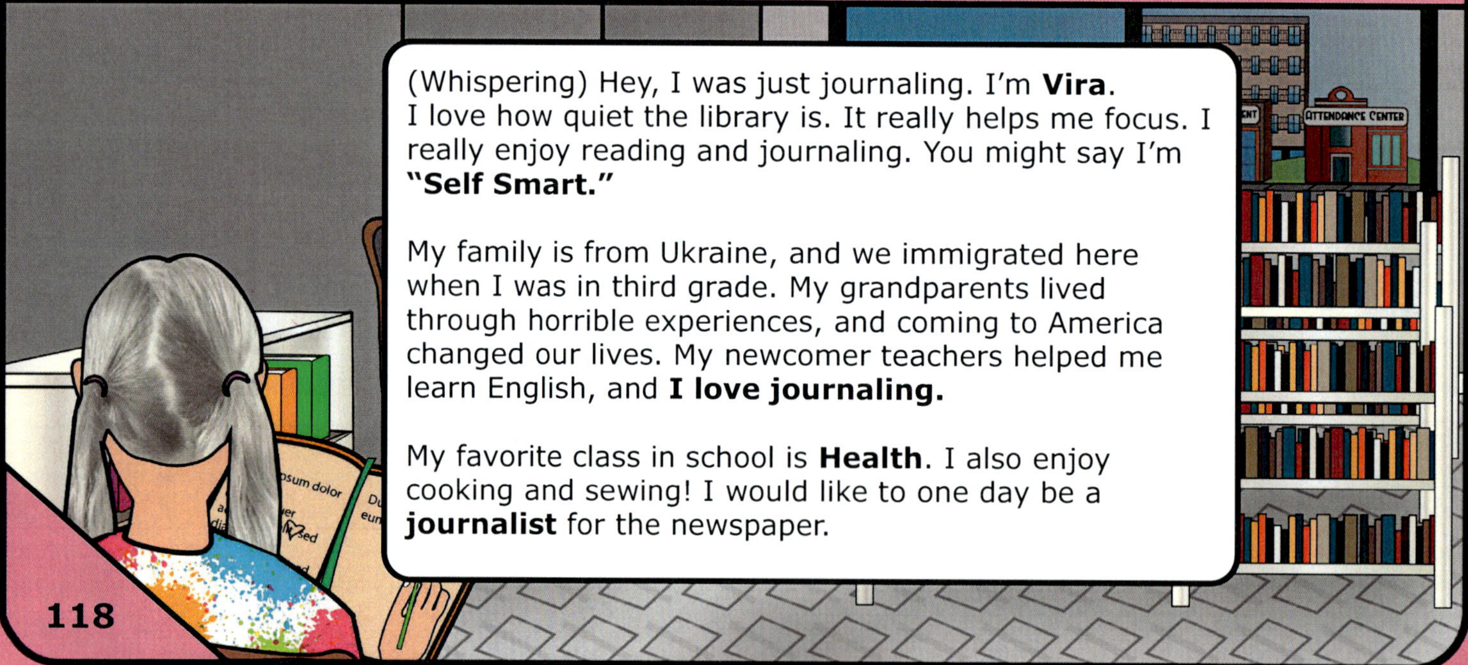

Here are some areas where you would see this type of intelligence:

- Journaling
- Reading
- Meditation (shh)
- Self-Talk
- Goal Setting
- Self-Care
- Prioritizing (1st 2nd 3rd 4th 5th)
- Instructions (1, 2, 3, 4)
- Showing Empathy
- Relationships

Score your level of this intelligence! (Based on your age and skills)

1	2	3	4	5	6	7	8	9	10
Low				Medium				High	

"Self Smart" Example Careers Checklist

- ☐ Author ☐ Cook ☐ Counselor ☐ Entrepreneur ☐ Farmer
- ☐ Historian ☐ Inventor ☐ Librarian ☐ Life Coach ☐ Manager
- ☐ Mentor ☐ Motivational Speaker ☐ Philosopher ☐ Trainer
- ☐ Planner ☐ Psychologist ☐ Researcher ☐ Writer

Your Interpersonal Intelligence:

This is the ability to recognize and understand other people's thoughts and feelings, allowing for strategic and effective communication.

"People Smart"

Can you share one person you would consider a friend?

Hey, it was great talking to you. Okay. See you later!" Oh, hey, I'm **Rishi**. I was just talking with a friend. I try to stay connected! My mom says I'm **"People Smart."** What can I say, I know how to talk to people.

I'm an only child, so my parents really encourage me to **be social.** I just started middle school and signed up for like three different clubs to be part of. I even got permission to invite a few friends over this weekend. It's gonna be a blast!

One of the elective classes I picked this year is **Speech**. We practice sharing information there, and I'm getting even better at what I do best.
I want to be a **mayor** someday!

Here are some areas where you would see this type of intelligence:

Working in Teams	Leadership	Time with Friends	Settling Conflict	Business
Giving a Speech	Coaching	Parties	Teaching	Talking on the Phone

Score your level of this intelligence! (Based on your age and skills)

1	2	3	4	5	6	7	8	9	10
Low				Medium				High	

"People Smart" Example Careers Checklist

- ☐ Business Sales ☐ Charity Organizer ☐ Comedian
- ☐ Content Creator ☐ Coordinator ☐ Counselor ☐ Journalist
- ☐ Nurse ☐ Police Officer ☐ Politician ☐ Recruiter
- ☐ Secretary ☐ Teacher ☐ Travel Agent ☐ Waiter

Your Existential Intelligence:

This describes a person's ability to consider the meaning and purpose of life and how it connects to other aspects of their life.

"Meaning Smart"

Can you share one things that is important to you?

Well, hello. I'm **Jack**. I turned 17 last month and recently got a job at the courthouse. I like being where the important stuff is happening. Sometimes I get to overhear parts of trials, and the reasoning behind each case feels like a blend of truth and art. I feel like I'm **"Meaning Smart."**

When my brother and I were in elementary school, we got really into ancient history. We'd make up adventures in the forest behind our house. I love stories that **dig into the "why" behind things**, each character has their own reasons for what they do.

History class is one of my favorites. Our teacher has us examine the politics of the time, and the debates we have can be pretty entertaining. I want to be a **professor**!

Here are some areas where you would see this type of intelligence:

Law and Justice	The History of the Earth	Human Life	Traditions	Death & Afterlife (RIP)
Meditation (Hmm ...)	Marriage	Stewardship	The Universe	Identity & Worship "Who am I?"

Score your level of this intelligence! (Based on your age and skills)

1	2	3	4	5	6	7	8	9	10
Low				Medium				High	

"Meaning Smart" Example Careers Checklist

- ☐ Author ☐ Chaplain ☐ Charity Organization ☐ Critic
- ☐ Ethicist ☐ Historian ☐ Human Rights Activist ☐ Judge
- ☐ Lawyer ☐ Philosopher ☐ Politician ☐ Public Speaker
- ☐ Scientist ☐ Social Justice ☐ Theologian

Self Smart

How do you usually know how you're feeling?

How does understanding yourself help you make decisions?

People Smart

Share about a time you helped someone?

Why are relationships important? Give an Example!

Meaning Smart

How do you decide what is right or wrong?

Who is someone you trust to help you when making big life decisions? Why?

Character

These intelligences help you manage yourself, your choices, and how you treat others. Relationships are a big part of life, and these intelligences help you interact with people in healthy and positive ways.

It is amazing how all of our **intelligences** come together to help make us the unique people we are.
M.A.X
Through your life you will continue to grow in different ways. Let's take a look at your strongest intelligences!

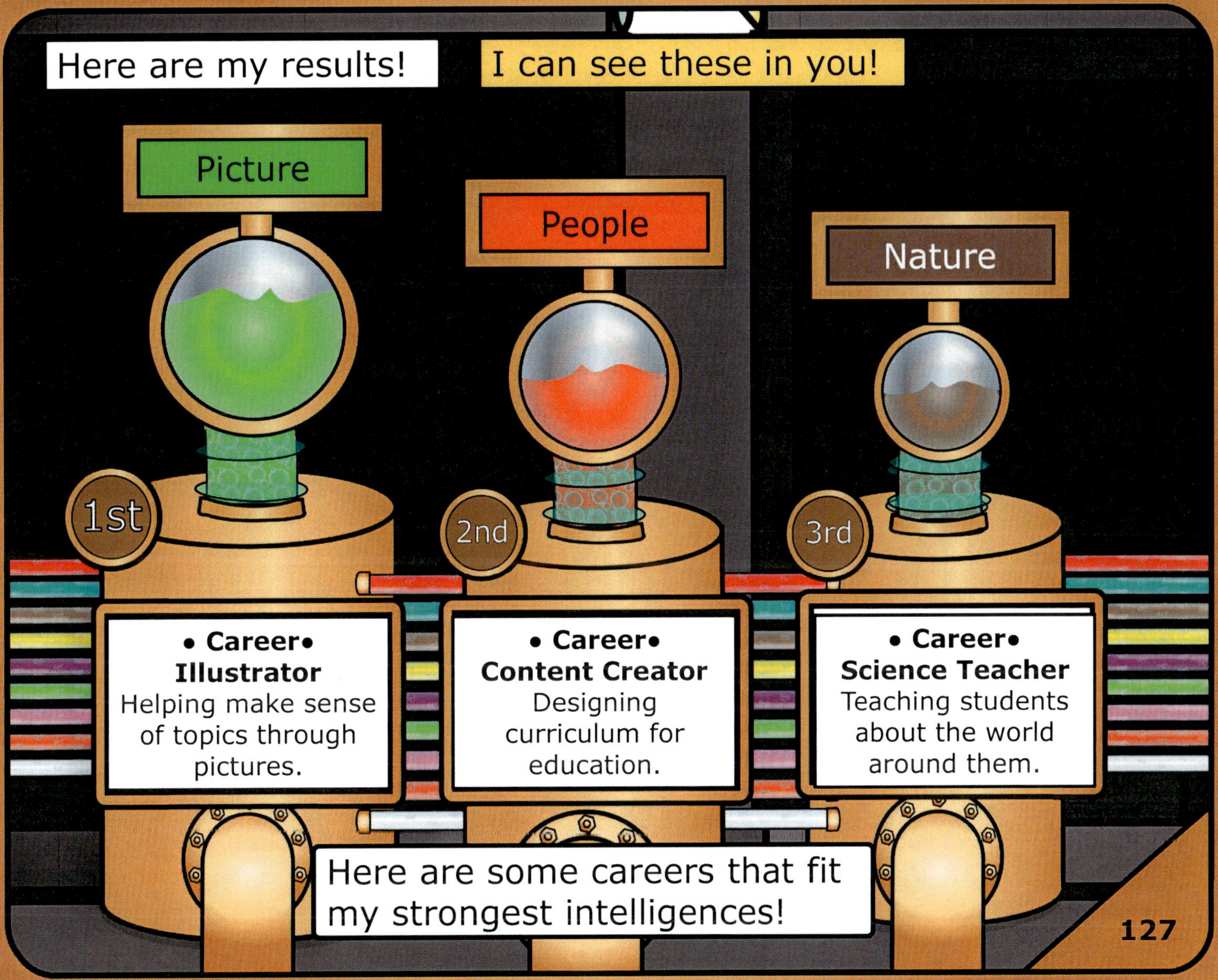
Here are my results!
I can see these in you!
Picture
People
Nature
1st
2nd
3rd
• Career•
Illustrator
Helping make sense of topics through pictures.
• Career•
Content Creator
Designing curriculum for education.
• Career•
Science Teacher
Teaching students about the world around them.
Here are some careers that fit my strongest intelligences!

What were your results!

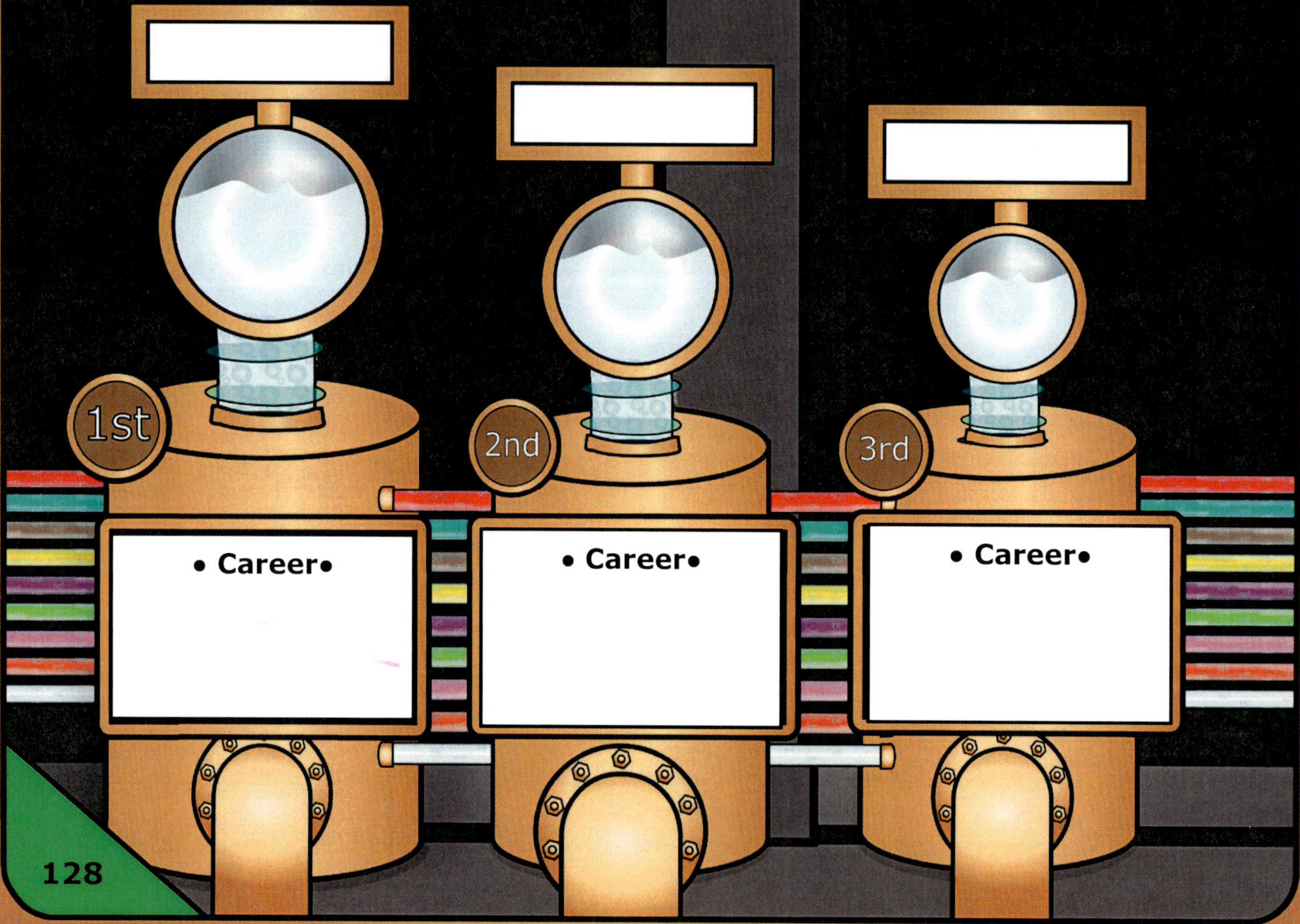

Next we are going to **research a career** that uses this type of intelligence! You might need a computer to find some important information!
Research!
Task:
Pay:
DT-7C

Research!

What is a career that you would be interested in?

Career

Why did you pick this?

What intelligences does this career use often?

Next let's learn more about this career: Tasks, Pay, Education, Location, Future and Skills.

Task:

What are some of the daily tasks for someone in this career?

Pay:

What is the average pay for this job?

In your state:

Nationwide:

Education:

What kind of education or training do you need to get this job? (Degree or program?)

Location:

What kind of environment does this job take place in: (office, outdoors, lab, etc.)

Do people in this job travel, or do they work in one place?

Future:

Is this career expected to grow in the future?

Skills:

What skills can I learn to prepare for this job? Why?

Great job! Thankfully you don't need to find a job tomorrow, but thinking about the future can help you to get the job you want!

That was the last task! Hey it looks like the storm has passed. **Hopefully after all our time here we understand ourselves better. Understand yourself helps you to better understand other.** Each of us are different and that is a good thing because together we can do so much more!
It has been a pleasure getting to know each one of you and your unique knowledge and skills. I will miss having you around!
Beep-Beep!

Beep-Beep!

To wrap up let's think through what we learned and how that will help you on your earning journey!

What have you learned about your **identity** that will help you to pick a career in the future?

What have you learned about your **personality** that will help you to pick a career in the future?

What have you learned about your **intelligence** that will help you to pick a career in the future?

Step 4:
Connect your multiple intelligences with a future career.

Now that you've done some research, try asking the adults in your life about their careers! You might be surprised to learn about their earning journeys!

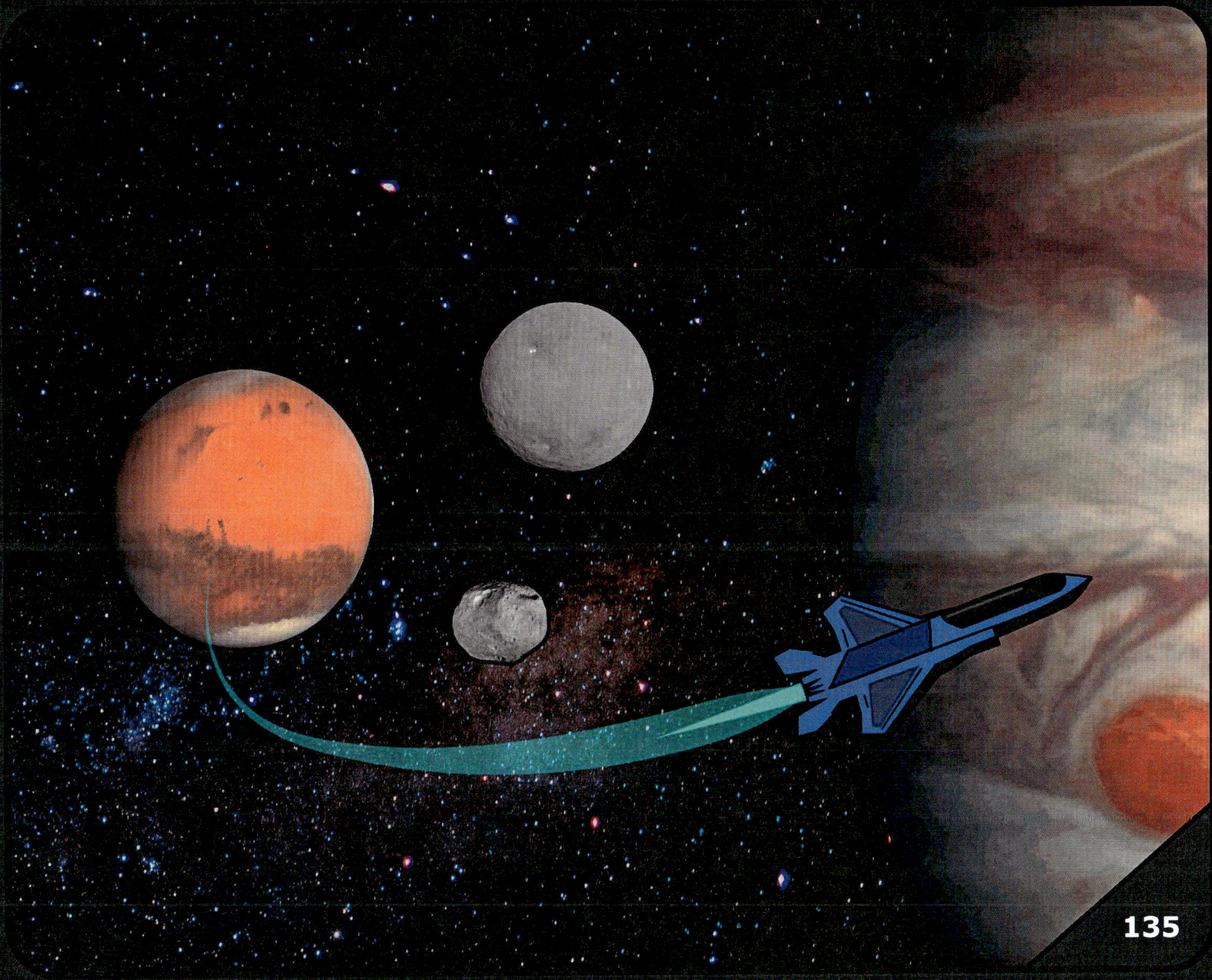

Thank you so much for joining us on this journey!
DT-7G

Let's look back at your journey. Did you meet your goals?

Step 1:
Describe a person's earning journey.

Step 2:
Study identity and identify how you see it guiding your life.

Step 3:
Recognize your personality and how it shapes your choices.

Step 4:
Connect your multiple intelligences with a future career.

Our Goal:
Study the connection between **identity**, **personality** and **work**.

Did we meet our goal? Why or why not?

A Career is when you help out at home. True or False?

What is the answer?

True

False

Which of these parts of your identity can you control?

What is the answer?

Race

Friends

Time Period

Economy

How has your personality shaped the way you like to do things? Give an example!

Journal ...

In this lesson, you explored **work and how it shaped by your identity, personality and intelligences**. Knowing yourself gives you the best chance of finding great work!

How do you think growing in these areas could make your life better?

Job Shadow

Make a checklist of people you could watch work their job.

- This could be at home, working on tasks around the house.
- This could be a job where they punch in for a shift. Just stay for a couple hours.
- This could be a career where they have an office you sit in and watch.

Explore the Store!

Next time you're at The Store:

- Play a game where you see who can identify more jobs at that place.
- Try to guess what education, skills or training that job would require.
- The winner gets a treat!

Mind & Money!

Chores are no Bore!

- When doing chores this week listen to music or an audiobook.
- Think of creative ways to make chores more fun this week!

The Game of Life

This game walks a person through education, work and growing a family. It is a great game to get discussions going about what you want in life.

- There is so much freedom in your future life choices!

The Galactic Growth journey will continue!
Until we meet again, take care and spread kindness everywhere!

A Career is when you help out at home. True or False?

False

Chores are where you help out at home. A career is work that you want to do for a long period of time and usually requires education, training and skills to get.

Which of these parts of your identity can you control?

Friends

The people that you choose to have around you will shape you. Your friends help you to make choices and encourage you as you grow up!

How has your personality shaped the way you like to do things? Give an example!

Every personality is different and will shape how you do things. For myself, I love being creative and for me that means being very flexible and figuring things out as I go. This can be really fun but also frustrating if I get stuck, then I have to take a break.

What's next?

You can continue the journey by joining us for the rest of the series. You rock for making your knowledge about **mind** & **money** a priority!

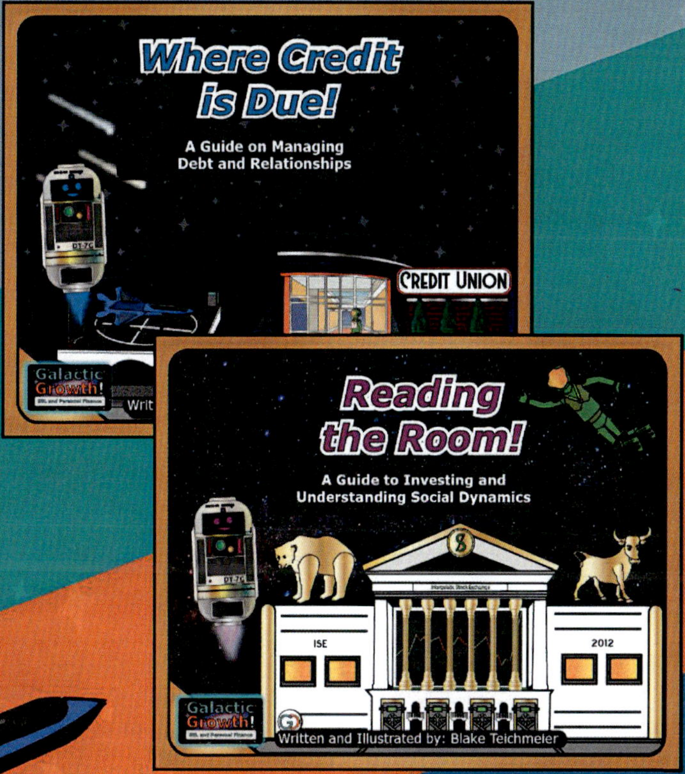

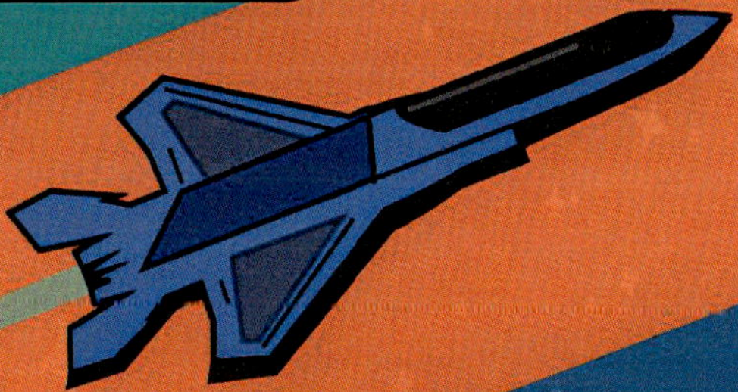

Glossary

Here you can find all of the major terms discussed in this book!

BIRTH	**52**	The parts of your identity you had no choice in: Body, Income at birth, Race, Time Period and Location.
Bodily Kinesthetic intelligence	**110**	This is the ability to understand and control your body's movements and abilities.
Career	**24**	A career is a path of work you choose that offers opportunities for growth and advancement over time.
CHOOSE	**56**	The parts of your identity you can choose: Careers, Hobbies, Opportunities, Outlooks, Social and Education.
Chores	**14**	Regular tasks done at home to help out, typically without pay.
Commission	**37**	You are paid based on the number of items or services you provide. For example, getting paid for each item you sell.
Consumers	**90**	The people who buy and use goods and services.
Existential Intelligence	**122**	This describes a person's ability to consider the meaning and purpose of life and how it connects to other aspects of their life.
Extravert	**68**	This is when you get energy from the outside world. Doing things with others recharges your energy.
Feelings	**76**	This is when a person relies on their feelings and values when making decisions.
Goods	**90**	Things you can buy and own.
Human Capital	**16**	The skills, knowledge, and experience a person has that make them valuable in work and life.
Identity	**46**	Who you are and how you see yourself. It shapes the way you understand the world around you.
Income	**18**	The money that a person earns from working, investments, or assistance.
Interpersonal Intelligence	**120**	This is the ability to recognize and understand other people's thoughts and feelings, allowing for strategic and effective communication.
Intrapersonal Intelligence	**118**	This is the ability to understand and analyze your own thoughts and emotions.

Intuition	**72**	This is when you trust ideas, patterns, and thinking to understand the world. Big idea people.
Job	**20**	Work for the purpose of making money.
Judging	**80**	This is where you want decisions to be made. You don't like it when things are unresolved, unfinished, or unplanned.
Linguistic Intelligence	**104**	This is the ability to understand and interpret words, then use them to express ideas clearly.
Mathematical Intelligence	**102**	This is the ability to understand and solve logical and mathematical problems.
Musical Intelligence	**112**	This is the ability to hear and recognize different parts of music and to reproduce those sounds with your voice or an instrument.
Naturalistic Intelligence	**106**	This is the ability to recognize and understand processes in the natural world.
Needs	**90**	Things you must have to stay alive and stay safe.
Perceiving/ Prospecting	**80**	This is where you want life to be flexible and spontaneous. You like adjusting to changes.
Personality	**46**	The way you think, feel, and act. It's what makes you unique and influences how you respond to the world.
Producers	**90**	The people who make goods and provide services.
Salary	**39**	You are paid based on a contract that outlines the work and pay. For example, you agree to do a specific job for a set amount of money.
Self-Awareness	**45**	The ability to understand yourself, including who you are, how you act, and how you feel.
Sensing/Observant	**72**	This is when you trust your hands-on experience to understand the world. Get into the details people.
Services	**90**	Actions or activities that someone does for you.
Spatial Intelligence	**114**	This is the ability to visualize and understand dimensions, directions, and shapes.
The Multiple Intelligences	**97**	This is the theory that there are multiple types of intelligence that a person can learn.
Thinking	**76**	This is when a person relies on their reason and logic when making decisions.
VIBE	**60**	The parts of your identity shaped by your culture: Norms, Ideals on Success, Community and Economy.
Wage:	**30**	You are paid based on the amount of time you work. For example, you may be paid by the hour.
Wants	**90**	Things you would like but could live without.

Check us out at
Teacher Pay Teachers

GreatCents.org

Our mission is to offer high-quality financial education resources for students at an affordable price. We invite you to explore our wide range of resources: lessons, games, foldables, and books. Thank you for your support!

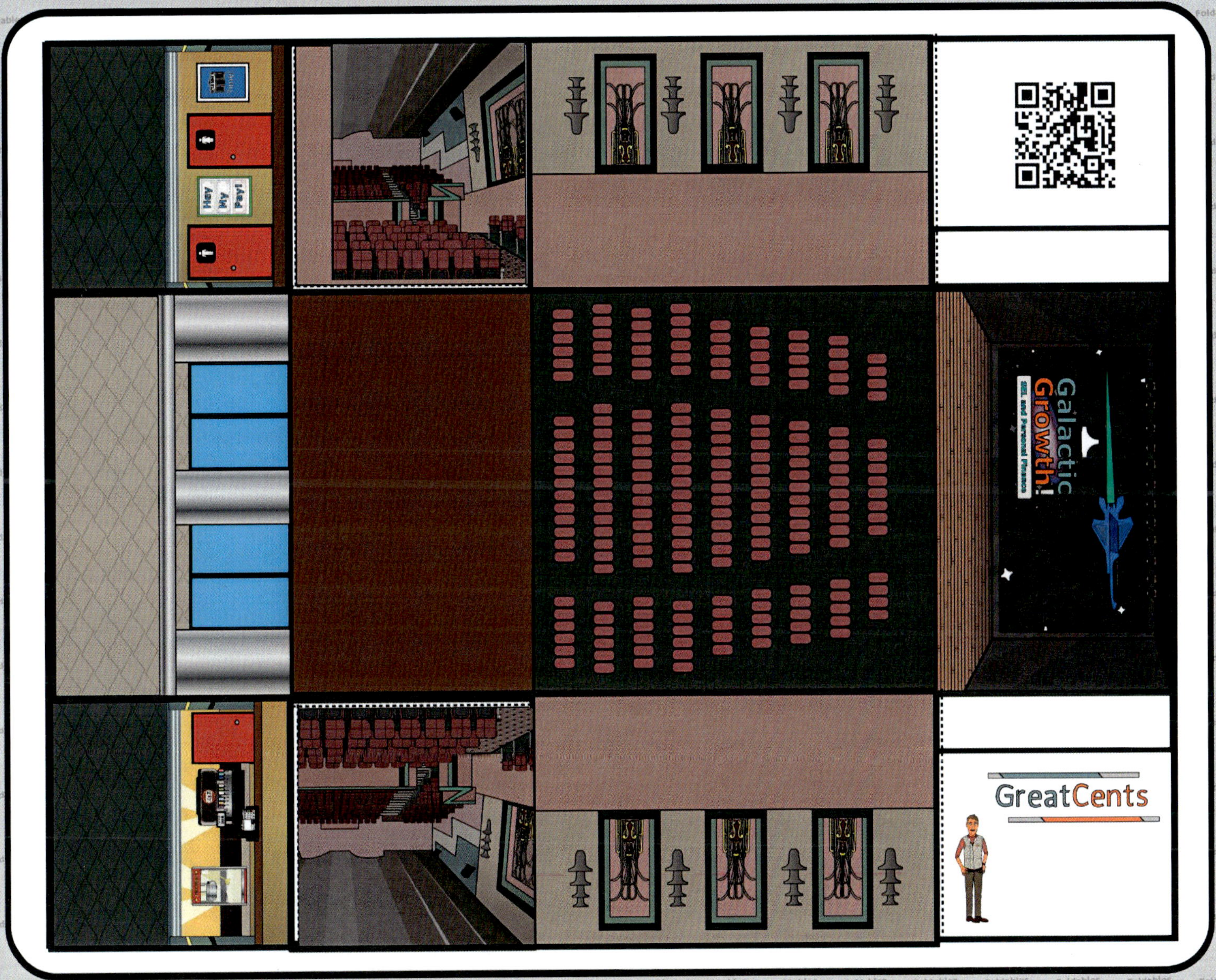
Hey My Pal!
Galactic Growth!
SEL and Personal Finance
GreatCents

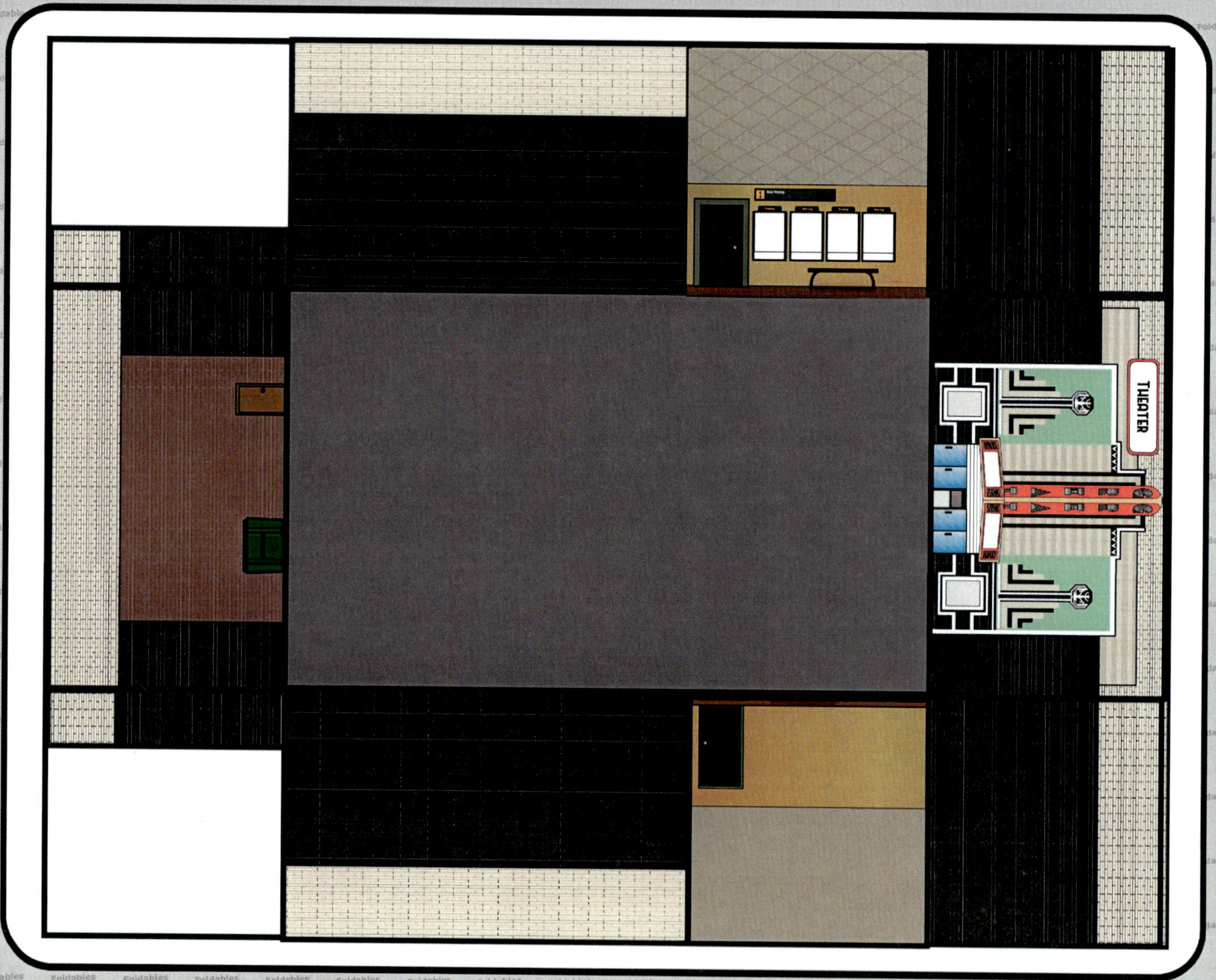
THEATER

Made in United States
North Haven, CT
04 November 2026

21730134R00086